Frederic Bateman

On Aphasia

Loss of Speech And the Localisation of the Faculty of Articulate Language

Frederic Bateman

On Aphasia
Loss of Speech And the Localisation of the Faculty of Articulate Language

ISBN/EAN: 9783744759021

Printed in Europe, USA, Canada, Australia, Japan

Cover: Foto ©ninafisch / pixelio.de

More available books at **www.hansebooks.com**

ON

A P H A S I A,

OR

Loss of Speech,

AND

THE LOCALISATION OF THE FACULTY OF ARTICULATE
LANGUAGE.

BY

FREDERIC BATEMAN, M.D., M.R.C.P.,

Physician to the Norfolk and Norwich Hospital.

LONDON: JOHN CHURCHILL AND SONS;
NORWICH: JARROLD AND SONS.
1870.

TO

HIS COLLEAGUES

THE PHYSICIANS AND SURGEONS

OF

THE NORFOLK AND NORWICH HOSPITAL,

𝔗𝔥𝔢𝔰𝔢 𝔓𝔞𝔤𝔢𝔰 𝔞𝔯𝔢 𝔍𝔫𝔰𝔠𝔯𝔦𝔟𝔢𝔡,

WITH EVERY FEELING OF RESPECT AND

FRIENDSHIP,

BY

THE AUTHOR.

PREFACE.

THE purpose of this little treatise is to bring together, in a convenient form, all the information I could obtain relative to a subject which has of late years engrossed so large a share of the attention, not only of the medical profession, but of scientific men generally, in all parts of the world—the localization of speech, and the causes which interfere with the proper manifestation of that faculty.

The different parts of this essay have already appeared, at certain intervals, in the pages of the *Journal of Mental Science*, and it is in deference to the opinion of those whose judgment I am bound to respect, that I now venture to publish them in a collected form.

If I have failed to contribute anything towards bridging the chasm which separates matter from mind, my researches will, at all events, tend to shew how little we really know about that wonderful piece of mechanism—the human brain.

FREDERIC BATEMAN.

Norwich, May, 1870.

CONTENTS.

APHASIA,

OR

Loss of Speech,

AND

The Localisation of the Faculty of Articulate Language.

PART I.

Aphasia is the term which has recently been given to the loss of the faculty of articulate language, the organs of phonation and of articulation, as well as the intelligence, being unimpaired. The pathology of this affection is at the present time the subject of much discussion in the scientific world; the French Academy devoted several of their *séances* during the year 1865 to its special elucidation, and the Medical Journals of France and of our own country have lately contained a good deal of original matter bearing upon this obscure feature in cerebral pathology.

In a short paper published in the "Lancet" for May 20, 1865, I drew attention to the existing state of our knowledge of the pathology of aphasia; since that period I have had occasion to make researches among various British and foreign authors, and having

B

noticed a certain number of curious observations bearing upon this interesting subject, I have thought it not
a useless task in this short essay to give a *résumé* of the
labours of scientific observers in various parts of the
world, who are endeavouring to elucidate this complex
question, adding thereunto the result of my own personal experience, the clinical history of my own cases
being given with a considerable amount of detail.

From time immemorial loss of speech, unconnected
with any other paralytic symptom, must have been
noticed; but it is only of late that the diagnostic value
of this symptom has been recognised, and its pathology
attempted to be explained; and it is probable that early
observers may have confounded paralysis of the tongue
from disease of the hypoglossus, with that loss of the
memory of words, and inability to give expression to
the thoughts which characterise aphasia.

It has been stated that Hippocrates confounded
aphasia with aphonia; I am inclined, however, to think
that the reputation of the Father of Medicine has
suffered from the fault of his English translator, for
in his ' Epidemics '* he describes a disease characterised
by *sore throat and hoarseness of voice*, using the phrase
" πολλοὶ φάρυγγας ἐπόνησαν φωναὶ κακούμεναι," the last two
words of which have been erroneously rendered in
English "*loss of speech!*" In another place Hippocrates
clearly distinguishes between loss of speech and loss of
voice, by employing the words " ἄναυδος" and " ἄφωνος"
in the description of the same case.

The following passage from Sauvages shows that the
distinction was clearly understood by him: "Aphonia

* 'Hippoc. de Morb. Pop.,' lib. iii, sec. ii, p. 80, edit. Innys.

est plenaria vocis suppressio. Mutitas (quibusdam alalia) est impotentia voces articulatas edendi, seu sermonem proferendi."

As this subject has more particularly engaged the attention of French pathologists during the last few years, it is most convenient to consider first their researches.

The minute anatomy of the surface of the brain not being to my knowledge described in any English author with the same amount of detail as occurs in M. Broca's description, I have condensed the following account from his work, "Sur le Siége de la Faculté du Langage Articulé."

The anterior lobe of the brain comprises all that part of the hemisphere situated above the fissure of Sylvius which separates it from the temporo-sphenoidal lobe, and in front of the furrow of Rolando, which divides it from the parietal lobe. The direction of the furrow of Rolando is nearly transverse; starting from the interhemispheric median fissure, it descends almost in a direct course, but with some slight flexuosities, terminating below and outside of the fissure of Sylvius, which it meets almost at a right angle, behind the posterior border of the lobe of the insula; in front this furrow is bounded by the transverse frontal convolution, and behind by the transverse parietal convolution.

The anterior lobe is composed of two stories or divisions, one inferior or orbital, formed by several convolutions called *orbital*, which lie on the roof of the orbit; the other superior, situated beneath the frontal and under the most anterior part of the parietal. This superior division of the anterior lobe is composed of four

fundamental convolutions called the *frontal convolutions;*
of these, one is posterior, the others are anterior. The
posterior, slightly tortuous, forms the anterior boundary
of the furrow of Rolando; it is therefore almost transverse and ascends from without inwards from the fissure
of Sylvius to the great median fissure which receives
the falx cerebri; it has been variously described as the
posterior, transverse, or ascending frontal convolution. The
three other convolutions of the superior division are
very tortuous and complicated; they have all an antero-
posterior direction, and, running side by side, extend
from before backwards over the whole length of the
frontal lobe, terminating behind at the tranverse frontal,
into which convolution they all three enter; they are
distinguished by the names of *first, second,* and *third
frontal convolutions.* The first and second frontal convolutions call for no special remark, but the precise
relations of the third are important. This convolution,
by its superior border, is contiguous to the second frontal
in its whole length; in reference to its inferior border,
the anterior half is in contact with the most external
orbital convolution, whereas the posterior half is free,
and forms the superior border of the fissure of Sylvius,
which separates it from the temporo-sphenoidal lobe.
In consequence of this latter relation, the third frontal
is sometimes called the *superior marginal convolution,* the
name of *inferior marginal* being given to the superior
convolution of the temporo-sphenoidal lobe, which forms
the inferior border of the fissure of Sylvius.

In drawing asunder these two convolutions which
bound the fissure of Sylvius, the lobe of the insula is
exposed, which covers the extra-ventricular nucleus of
the corpus striatum. The result of these relations is,

that a lesion which is propagated from the frontal to the temporo-sphenoidal lobe, or *vice versâ*, will pass almost necessarily by the lobe of the insula, and from thence, in all probability, it will extend to the extra-ventricular nucleus of the corpus striatum, seeing that the proper substance of the insula which separates the nucleus from the surface of the brain is composed of only a very thin layer.*

As far back as 1825 Bouillaud placed the faculty of articulation in the frontal lobes of the brain, which he considered to be the organs of the formation of words and of memory; and he stated that the exercise of thought demanded the integrity of these lobes; he also collected 114 observations of disease of the anterior lobes accompanied by lesion of the faculty of speech.

Andral, who has investigated the subject very fully, analysed 37 cases, observed by himself and others, of lesion of one or both of the anterior lobes, and found that speech was abolished 21 times, and retained 16 times; when the lesion was unilateral, however, he has not stated on which side the morbid condition existed. He has also collected 14 cases where speech was abolished without any alteration in the anterior lobes, but where the lesion existed in the middle or in the posterior lobes. He cites the case of a woman, eighty years of age, who, three years before entering the hospital, was suddenly deprived of speech, without lesion of the intelligence, motion, or sensation, and still retaining the power of walking about; she presented, however, signs of organic disease of the heart, and died at last

* Vide Plate facing title page.

of pulmonary apoplexy. At the necropsy there was found in the left hemisphere, softening of cerebral substance on a level with, and external to, the posterior extremity of the corpus striatum; and in the right hemisphere, a similar softening at the junction of the anterior and posterior half of the hemisphere.*

Then comes Dr. Dax, who places the lesion exclusively in the *left* hemisphere; basing his theory on the fact that when the subjects of aphasia are at the same time hemiplegic, the paralysis is always on the *right* side, his essay containing no less than 140 observations in support of his views.

His son, Dr. G. Dax, following in the wake of his father, wrote an essay, in which, whilst confirming the theory as to the lesion being in the left hemisphere, he localised it more especially in the anterior and external part of the middle lobe.

The *ne plus ultra* of pathological topography, however, was reserved to M. Broca, who defines the seat of lesion in aphasia to be "*the posterior part of the third frontal convolution of the left hemisphere!*" M. Broca's views are detailed at some length in the proceedings of the Paris Anatomical Society for 1861, and the following is a brief summary of the two cases upon which he has founded his somewhat startling theory.

A man named Leborgne, 50 years of age, and epileptic, was admitted into the surgical ward of M. Broca, at Bicêtre, for phlegmonous erysipelas, occupying the whole of the right lower limb. When M. Broca questioned him about the origin of his disorder, he only answered by the monosyllable "Tan," repeated

* 'Clinique Médicale,' chap. iv, observ. xvii.

twice, and accompanied by a gesture of the left hand. On making inquiries, it transpired that this man had been an inmate of the hospital in another wing for twenty-one years; that he had been the subject of epilepsy since infancy; that he had followed the occupation of a lastmaker up to the age of thirty, when he lost his speech, but no information could be elicited as to whether the loss of speech had come on suddenly, or had been ushered in by any other symptom.

On his admission at Bicêtre he is stated to have been intelligent, understanding all that was said to him, and differing from a perfectly healthy man only in the loss of the faculty of articulate language; for whatever question was put to him, he invariably answered by the monosyllable "Tan," which, with the exception of a coarse oath ("*S— n— de D—*"), composed his vocabulary. At the end of ten years, a new symptom showed itself in weakness in the motor power of the right arm, which gradually resulted in complete paralysis of the right side, and he had already been bedridden seven years when the occurrence of a surgical complication rendered it necessary to transfer him to the ward of M. Broca, who, in describing his *then* condition, states that there was no distortion of face, the tongue was protruded straight, the movements of that organ being perfectly free in every direction; mastication was unimpaired, but deglutition was effected with some difficulty, this being however due to commencing paralysis of the pharynx, and not to paralysis of the tongue, for it was only the third period of deglutition which was difficult; the voice was natural, and the functions of the bladder and rectum unimpaired.

The patient having died in six days, a careful post-

mortem examination was made, when all the viscera
were found healthy, with the exception of the encephalon;
the muscles of the right upper and lower extremities,
however, were in an advanced stage of fatty degeneration
and shrivelled up.   The bones of the cranium were
somewhat increased in density, the dura mater thickened
and very vascular, the pia mater considerably injected
in certain places, and everywhere thickened, opaque, and
infiltrated with yellowish plastic matter of the colour of
pus, but which, examined under the microscope, did not
contain any pus-globules.   The greater part of the
frontal lobe of the left hemisphere was softened, and
the destruction of cerebral substance had resulted in a
cavity of the size of a hen's egg and filled with serum ;
the cavity was situated upon a level with the fissure of
Sylvius, and was caused by the destruction of the inferior marginal convolution of the temporo-sphenoidal
lobe, the convolutions of the island of Reil, and the
subjacent part or extra-ventricular nucleus of the corpus
striatum.   In the frontal lobe the inferior part of the
frontal transverse convolution was destroyed, as also the
posterior half of the *second and third frontal convolutions*,
the loss of substance being most apparent however in
the third frontal convolution.   The weight of the
encephalon after the evacuation of the fluid filling the
cavity did not exceed 987 grammes (35 ounces), being
less by 400 grammes (14 ounces) than the average
weight of the brain in men of fifty years of age.

   M. Broca then compares the result of the autopsy
with the clinical observations during life; he considers
that the primary seat of mischief was probably in the
third frontal convolution extending gradually to the
others, and that this process of disorganisation corres-

ponded to the first stage of the clinical history, which lasted ten years, and during which period the faculty of speech alone was abolished, all the other functions of the body being intact; the second stage, which lasted eleven years, and which was characterised clinically by partial paralysis, and then complete hemiplegia, he connects with the extension of the disease to the island of Reil and to the extra-ventricular nucleus of the corpus striatum.

A man, aged 84, formerly a labourer, was admitted into the surgical ward at Bicêtre on the 27th October, 1861, for a fracture of the neck of the femur. This man had been received into the hospital eight years before for senile debility, there being at that time no paralysis, and the organs of special sense and the intelligence being unimpaired. In the month of April, 1860, whilst descending a staircase he fell, suddenly became unconscious, and was treated for what was considered to be an attack of apoplexy; in a few days he was convalescent, there never having been the least symptom of paralysis of limbs, but since the fit he had suddenly and definitely lost the faculty of speech, being only able to pronounce certain words articulated with difficulty; his intelligence had received no appreciable shock; he understood all that was said to him, and his brief vocabulary, accompanied by an expressive mimic, enabled him to be understood by those who lived habitually with him. He continued in this condition up to the time of the accident which caused him to be transferred to the surgical ward under the care of M. Broca, to whose questions he only answered by signs, accompanied by one or two syllables pronounced hastily and with visible effort. These syllables had a definite meaning, and consisted of the following French words—"*oui, non, tois* (for *trois*), and *toujours*." He also possessed a fifth word, which he only pronounced when he was asked his name, he then answered "Lelo," for Lelong, which was his proper name. The three first words of his vocabulary corresponded each to a definite idea. When he wished to affirm or approve he said "*oui*," employing the word "*non*" to express the opposite idea. The word "*tois*" expressed all his ideas of numbers, but as he was aware it did not correctly convey his thoughts, he rectified the error by gesture: for instance, when asked how long he had been at Bicêtre, he answered *tois*, but raised eight fingers. When asked what was o'clock (it being then ten) he answered *tois*, and raised ten fingers. Whenever the three other words were not applicable, he invariably used the word *toujours*, which consequently for him had no definite meaning. There was no paralysis of the tongue, which was protruded straight, and was moveable in every direction, each half being of the same thickness; sight and hearing were good, deglutition was normal, and there was no paralysis of limbs, nor of the rectum or bladder.

M. Broca sums up the symptoms by calling attention to the following salient points: 1st, that the patient understood all that was said; 2nd, that he applied with discretion the four words of his vocabulary; 3rd, that his intelligence was unimpaired; 4th, that he understood numbers; 5th, that he had neither lost the general faculty of language nor the movement of the muscles concerned in phonation and articulation; and that therefore he had only lost the faculty of articulate

language. The patient died in twelve days. Autopsy.
—The bones of the cranium were somewhat thickened,
and all the sutures ossified; the dura mater was healthy;
the arachnoid cavity contained a considerable quantity
of serum; the pia mater was neither thickened nor
congested. The encephalon weighed, with its membranes, 1136 grammes (40 ounces), being far below the
average weight of that of adult males. The right
hemisphere, the cerebellum, the pons varolii, and the
medulla oblongata, were in a perfectly normal condition.
In the left hemisphere the lesion was limited to a loss
of substance in the *posterior third of the second and third
frontal convolutions*, a small cavity having been thus
formed which was filled with serum. The walls of the
cavity and the neighbouring cerebral tissue were firmer
than usual; there were present some little spots of an
orange-yellow colour, apparently of an hæmatic origin,
and microscopic examination revealed the presence of
blood crystals. The lesion then was clearly not softening, but the seat of a former apoplectic clot; and it will
be remembered that the patient suddenly lost his speech
in an attack of apoplexy eighteen months before his
death.

In alluding to the above two cases, M. Broca says
that in the first case—that of Leborgne—it is only by
comparing the different stages of the disease as observed
during life with the post-mortem appearances, that he
assumes the high probability of the lesion having
commenced in the third frontal convolution; but in the
second case—that of Lelong—there being no other
symptom than loss of speech, and the lesion being
strictly limited to the second and third frontal con-

volutions, he considers the aphasia was incontestably
due to disease of that portion of the nervous centres.
Whilst admitting that two cases are insufficient to
resolve one of the most obscure and disputed questions
in cerebral pathology, M. Broca considers himself
justified in asserting that the integrity of the *third
frontal convolution* (and perhaps of the second) appears
indispensable to the exercise of the faculty of articulate
language.*

A later writer of the French School, Dr. J. Falret,
has collected from various authors no less than sixty-
two cases, in the arrangement of which he adopts the
following classification: 1st. All those cases in which
the patients, whilst retaining intelligence and integrity
of the organs of phonation, can only remember or
articulate spontaneously certain words or classes of
words, or even certain syllables or letters, but who can
repeat and write any word that may be suggested to
them by others. 2nd. Those in which the patients are
only able to pronounce spontaneously certain words,
syllables, or phrases always the same, not being however able to repeat other words dictated to them, although they retain the power of writing them; or if
the power of repeating words thus dictated be retained,
that of writing them is abolished. 3rd. Those more
rare cases in which the patients can only pronounce
certain words always the same, which, aided by gesture,
enable them to express their thoughts, the power of
reading, writing, and repeating words dictated, being
abolished. Dr. Falret admits that this classification is
artificial, and probably does not embrace all the varieties

* 'Sur le Siége de la Faculté du Langage Articulé,' p. 39.

met with in practice. After paying a just tribute to recent workers in this field of observation, he concludes his very elaborate essay with remarking:—"That the question of perverted speech and of loss of the memory of words in cerebral affections is not yet matured; that it is more complex and more extensive than at first sight appears; that it borders upon the most obscure and the most disputed points of cerebral pathology and of the physiology of language; and that fresh observations of a detailed character are indispensably necessary, and that all generalization and all absolute conclusions are, for the present, premature." *

Professor Trousseau has made this subject a prominent feature in his clinical lectures, where he details several most interesting cases in which, when hemiplegia existed, it was with one exception always on the right side.†

During several months of the session of 1865, the French Academy of Medicine became the arena for discussion upon this most interesting subject, in which many of the leading physicians and surgeons took a part. At one of these meetings M. Trousseau gave the result of his statistical researches, and stated that in 134 observations collected by himself, 124 were confirmatory of M. Dax's proposition of localizing the faculty of speech in the left hemisphere, and 10 were contrary. With regard to M. Broca's theory of attributing aphasia to a lesion of the third frontal convolution, he found that 14 cases were in favour of it, and 18 opposed to it; amongst the latter, he mentioned the case of a woman treated at La Salpêtrière by M.

* Des Troubles du Langage, p. 53.
† 'Clinique Médicale,' tom. ii, p. 571.

Charcot for right hemiplegia with aphasia, and where
after death there was found a lesion of the left insula,
and also of the third frontal convolution of the *right*
side.

M. Trousseau also cited a case observed by M. Peter,
the subject of which was a woman who had left hemiplegia, and who could only say, " *Oui, parbleu !* " who
died from the effects of senile gangrene, and at whose
autopsy a lesion was found of the third frontal convolution of the *right* side, also of the insula and of the
posterior part of the corpus striatum, there being also
embolism of the middle cerebral artery.   Here, says
M. Trousseau, are two cases of aphasia, with a lesion on
the *right* side.

At another of these discussions M. Velpeau alluded
to the fact of M. Bouillaud having offered many years
since a prize of 500 francs for any well authenticated
case in which the two anterior lobes were destroyed, or
more or less seriously injured, without speech being
affected, saying that he (M. Velpeau) should claim the
prize on the faith of the following case, with specimen,
which he presented to the Academy twenty-two years
ago.   In the month of March, 1843, a wigmaker, sixty
years of age, came under M. Velpeau's care for a disease of the urinary passages.   With the exception of
his prostatic disease, he seemed to be in excellent
health, was very lively, cheerful, full of repartee, and
evidently in possession of all his faculties; one remarkable symptom in his case being his *intolerable loquacity*.
A greater chatterer never existed; and on more than
one occasion complaints were made by the other patients
of their talkative neighbour, who allowed them rest
neither night nor day.   A few days after admission this

man died suddenly, and a careful autopsy was made, with the following results :—Hypertrophy of the prostate, with disease of the bladder. On opening the cranium a scirrhous tumour was found, which had taken the place of the two anterior lobes! Here then was a man who up to the time of his death presented no symptom whatever of cerebral disease, and who, far from having any lesion of the faculty of speech, was unusually loquacious, and who for a long period prior to his decease must have had a most grave disease of the brain, which had destroyed a great part of the anterior lobes.

During the protracted debates at the Academy of Medicine, the pathological and psychological aspects of the question were reviewed with great force and eloquence, but the discussion closed without this learned body having arrived at any definite decision in reference to the localization of the faculty of speech.

Several very interesting observations have been recorded in the French press, most of which are more or less corroborative of Broca's views, or at least of the association of loss of speech with lesion of the *left* hemisphere.

In the 'Gazette des Hôpitaux' for July 1st, 1865, Dr. Lesur mentions a remarkable case of a child, who, in consequence of a fracture of the frontal bone caused by a kick from a horse, was trepanned about one inch and a quarter above the left orbit. The child recovered, but during the progress of the treatment it was observed that pressure on the brain at the exposed part suspended the power of speech, which returned as soon as the pressure was removed.

Another case of traumatic aphasia has recently occurred in the practice of Dr. Castagnon, the subject of it being a young girl, aged 20, who was shot in the head, the accident resulting in a comminuted fracture of the antero-superior portion of the left parietal; although there was no depression of bone, several spiculæ were removed, and there was subsequently hernia cerebri and sphacelus of the protruded portion, which was removed by ligature. There was a comatose condition for six days, dextral paralysis and complete loss of speech for a month, at the end of which time she could speak, her vocabulary, however, being limited to four phrases, "*Mon Dieu! Jesus! mon père, ma mère.*" At the expiration of a year the paralysis had subsided, and the patient resumed her occupation, but although the intelligence was as perfect as before the accident, the young girl spoke but very little, and with great difficulty.*

An interesting case was observed a few months since at the Hospital St. Antoine by M. Jaccoud, the subject being a man aged 44, suffering from Bright's disease, who, without any premonitory symptom, suddenly became aphasic, there being no other paralytic symptom except a limited facial paralysis. The aphasia was of short duration, and at the end of five weeks he spoke nearly as well as before, but soon sank from disease of the kidneys. At the post-mortem there was observed fatty degeneration of both kidneys; insufficiency of the mitral valve, which was covered with small vegetations; the arteries of the circle of Willis were healthy, and there was no disease of the grey matter of the convolutions, but there was a limited and well-defined softening

* 'Gazette des Hôpitaux,' Oct. 12, 1867.

of the white substance in the immediate neighbourhood of the third frontal convolution of the left anterior lobe, great stress being laid on the fact that the convolution itself was in nowise affected.[*]

Professor Béhier, in a clinical lecture recently delivered at the Hôtel Dieu, mentioned the case of a woman who was admitted into one of his wards with right hemiplegia, the result of cerebral hæmorrhage; and in whom, one of the first symptoms following the effusion was aphasia, which assumed in her case a very exceptional form. This woman was born in Italy, and had resided both in Spain and France; of the three languages she had thus acquired, she had completely forgotten the Italian and Spanish, and had only retained a most limited use of French, in which language *she only repeated as an echo* the words pronounced in her presence, without, however, attaching any meaning to them.

In reference to the question of localisation, M. Béhier stated, that after analysing the cases observed during the last few years, as well as those recorded by Abercrombie, Rochoux, Lallemand, and Andral, he had collected 122 observations opposed to the theories of M. M. Bouillaud, Dax, and Broca; in 82 instances, lesion of the anterior lobes had been observed without aphasia, and in 34 cases, aphasia coincided with disease in other parts of the brain.[†]

The next three cases I have to mention are instances of the lesion of the third frontal convolution without aphasia; but as the lesion was on the *right* side, they

* Gazette des Hôpitaux, May 16, 1867.
† Ibid., March 20th, 1869.

C

may be adduced as *negative proofs* of the truth of M. Broca's theory.

M. Fernet has recorded a case of left hemiplegia without aphasia in a female aged 36, and at whose autopsy, the entire frontal lobe of the *right* hemisphere was found broken down by softening. In the 'Gazette Hebdomadaire' for July, 1863, M. Parrot relates a case of complete atrophy of the island of Reil and of the third frontal convolution on the *right* side, with preservation of the intelligence and of the faculty of articulate language. M. Charcot has recorded the case of a woman, 77 years of age, who had left hemiplegia without embarrassment of speech, or loss of the memory of words, and at whose autopsy there was found yellow softening of the surface of the *right* frontal lobe, the second and third frontal convolutions being completely destroyed, and there being no lesion of the central parts of the brain.

I need scarcely remark that cases like the three just mentioned, of lesion on the *right side without aphasia* are quite as valuable in a statistical point of view, and tend as much to settle the *quæstio vexata*, as cases where the converse condition exists, viz., lesion on the *left* side *with* aphasia.

I now arrive at a class of cases which have a directly opposite pathological signification to those above mentioned, the six following observations being all calculated to invalidate the recent theories as to the seat of articulate language.

M. Peter relates the case of a man who fractured his skull by a fall from a horse. After recovery from the initial stupor there succeeded a *remarkable loquacity*, although after death it was found that the two frontal lobes of the brain were reduced to a pulp (*réduits en bouillie*).

In Trousseau's 'Clinique Médicale,' the following case is recorded:—In the year 1825, two officers quartered at Tours quarrelled, and satisfied their honour by a duel, as a result of which one of them received a ball which entered at one temple and made its exit at the other. The patient survived six months without any sign of paralysis or of lesion of articulation, nor was there the least hesitation in the expression of his thoughts till the supervention of inflammation of the central substance which occurred shortly before his death, when it was ascertained that the ball had traversed the two frontal lobes at their centre.

M. Charcot, who has collected a number of observations more or less corroborative of M. Broca's assertions, has however recorded the case of a woman, aged 47, who from a fit of apoplexy suddenly became hemiplegic on the right side and aphasic. Her intelligence was unaffected, and memory reported as good, but her articulate language was reduced to the monosyllable "Ta," which she was in the habit of repeating several times over ("Ta, ta, ta, ta"), very rapidly and very distinctly, every time she tried to answer any question or to communicate her own ideas; the tongue was perfectly free, and could be moved in every direction. After death it was found that softening had destroyed the first and second convolutions of the temporosphenoidal lobe, the island of Reil, the extra-ventricular nucleus of the corpus striatum, and the intra-ventricular nucleus in its posterior half, the optic thalamas being intact; the frontal convolutions presented no alteration either in volume, colour, or consistence, the examination being conducted with the greatest care, and even in the presence of M. Broca, who frankly admitted this case to be at variance with his hypothesis.*

A woman, aged 73, was admitted into the Salpêtrière under M. Vulpian, her only symptom being loss of the power of speech, there was no paralysis of limbs, and M. Vulpian looked upon this patient as a type of aphasia. After a few days she became hemiplegic on the right side, and died of pneumonia five weeks after admission. At the autopsy softening was observed to a considerable extent in the posterior half of the supra-ventricular white matter of the left hemisphere, there being not the slightest indication of any lesion of the frontal or other convolutions; there was, however, obstruction of the left middle cerebral artery, caused partly by atheromatous thickening of the walls and partly by a fibrinous deposit evidently of a recent date, the result rather of a thrombosis than of an embolism.

A man, aged 42, was admitted into the Hôtel Dieu, under the care of M. Trousseau, on 25th March, 1865. The sister of the ward, deeming him to be in extreme danger, began to exhort him to think about his last moments, when she received for an answer, "*N'y a pas de danger.*" Soon afterwards the dresser arrived, and to his first question the patient replied, "*N'y a pas de danger.*" Second question, same answer. It was evident that the man was aphasic, and the discovery that there was paralysis of the right side of the body confirmed the diagnosis. There was marked rigidity of the right upper extremity, the forearm being

* Broca, op. cit., p. 6.

strongly flexed upon the arm; the tongue was protruded straight, and was freely moveable; the right half of the face was paralysed, but the orbicularis palpebrarum was unaffected. Some weeks after admission he seems to have forgotten his old formula, for to every question he answered, "*Tout de même.*" Death occurred after four months' residence in the hospital, when the necropsy gave the following results. Almost the entire left hemisphere was converted into a vast cavity, having the appearance of a true cyst, the walls of which were formed above by a very thin layer of cerebral matter flattened and even softened, and which was adherent to the much-thickened pia mater; in front and behind, all the remaining cerebral substance was yellowish and much softened. The orbital convolutions, the island of Reil, and the first and second frontal convolutions were in a perfectly normal condition; the third frontal convolution was pronounced healthy in that portion (the posterior third or half) which bordered the fissure of Sylvius and the furrow of Rolando, but it was evidently softened and almost destroyed in its upper part, where it was included in the general softening of the hemisphere, which also involved the corpus striatum and the thalamus opticus; the middle cerebral artery was not obliterated. This examination was made in the presence of Professors Trousseau and Guillot, and whilst showing the care with which this subject is being investigated by the French faculty, it possesses an additional interest from the fact that when the autopsy was completely finished and the brain mutilated by the successive slices that had been made, M. Broca arrived, and declared that the postero-external part of the third frontal convolution was yellow and softened, and that it had been thought healthy because it had been looked for where it did not exist !*

The last case to which I shall allude under this head is recorded by M. Langaudin of Nice, the subject of it being a soldier, who discharged the contents of a pistol through the mouth, the ball traversing the arch of the palate in the median line; the patient lived two months, *and speech was unaffected*, although after death it was found that the anterior lobe of the *left* hemisphere was entirely destroyed by suppuration.*

I conclude the history of the French contributions to the literature of aphasia by a brief allusion to Dr. Ladame's essay on lesions of speech in connection with tumours of the brain. From his researches it would seem that derangement of speech is not common in cerebral tumours, he having observed it only 44 times in 332 observations. According to Dr. Ladame's valuable statistics, tumours of the corpus striatum and of the pons varolii are more frequently attended by loss of speech than those occurring in any other part of the encephalon. He found that tumours in the *middle* lobes were more frequently accompanied by lesion of speech than those occupying the *anterior* lobes, in the proportion of five to four. These curious results have led Dr. Ladame to dissent from the doctrine which would place the seat of articulate language in the anterior lobes.

* 'Gazette des Hôpitaux,' Sept. 28, 1865.
† Ibid., April 29, 1865.

PART II.

From the brief summary I have given of the labours of the pathologists of the French school, it will be observed that the evidence deducible therefrom is of such a conflicting character, as to leave quite unsettled the complex question of the localisation of the faculty of speech. The history of the continental contributions to the literature of aphasia would, however, be very incomplete, without a brief glance at the researches of the German and Dutch physiologists.

Schrœder van der Kolk,* in his chapter on the accessory ganglia in the medulla oblongata, endeavours to establish a close physiological and pathological connection between the function of articulation and speech and the corpora olivaria. Besides citing numerous cases in illustration of his hypothesis, he gives an *a priori* reason for his theory in the fact that the corpora olivaria occur only in mammalia—that on comparing these organs as occurring among mammalia themselves, it is to be observed that they nowhere exist on so extensive a scale, and are so fully developed, or present so strongly plaited a corpus ciliare, as in man; that in

* On the Minute Structure and Functions of the Spinal Cord and Medulla Oblongata. Translated by Dr. W. D. Moore, p. 140.

the higher mammalia, as the apes, they are most like those in man, and that in man they exceed in circumference by two or three times those of the chimpanzee. To Van der Kolk, these circumstances are suggestive of the idea that in man the corpora olivaria have a much more important function to discharge than in animals; and as these bodies are connected by special fasciculi with the nuclei of the hypoglossus, he looks upon them as auxiliary ganglia of that nerve, and as such, joined to it for the production of special combinations of movement. He also suspects that the very delicate combinations of motion in the human tongue in articulation and speech, may afford an explanation of the much greater size of the olivary bodies, and of their more intimate connection with the nuclei of the hypoglossus. In support of these views, Van der Kolk cites several cases of impairment of the faculty of speech, in all of which there was found after death lesion or degeneration of the olivary bodies. Of these observations the limits of this essay will only permit me briefly to allude to one which seems to me to be particularly pertinent to the subject now under consideration :—

G. van A., aged 22, had been dumb from birth, but not deaf. She had always enjoyed good health, and although idiotic, usually understood all that was said to her; but had never been able to form an articulate sound, and only now and then uttered a squeak. The patient having died from the effects of diarrhœa, the following appearances were observed at the autopsy. On removing the hard, but thin and small skull, the cerebrum appeared small and ill-developed; the convolutions, especially on the anterior lobes, were slight and not numerous; in consequence of the diminished arching of the anterior lobes, the so-called convolutions of the third rank of Foville were very small, and scarcely shown on the inner longitudinal surface of the hemispheres; the convolutions on the posterior lobes were also but little developed. On the anterior lobes, beneath the os frontis, was seen a spot of the size of the palm of a small hand, and bloody exudation under the arachnoid, in which situation the pia mater was adherent to the cortical substance, which was in many parts softened. On section the grey and white substances were here and there thickly studded with red sanguineous points; the thalami optici presented a strikingly yellow colour; the pons Varolii was smaller and narrower than usual, and the corpora olivaria were unusually minute and slightly developed, being less than one third of the normal size.

Van der Kolk, in commenting on this case remarks: that as in this instance there was complete inability to articulate, and consequent absence of speech, without deafness and without proper paralysis of the tongue, which the patient could move, coinciding with an extremely defective development of the corpora olivaria; therefore the influence of these bodies on the complicated movements of the tongue in speech seemed scarcely to admit of doubt!

It will be observed that in laying great stress on the fact of the atrophy of the olivary bodies, the learned Utrecht Professor quite loses sight of the deductions to be drawn from the extremely imperfect development of the frontal convolutions, and also from the positive diseased condition of the anterior lobes; and it seems to me that both Bouillaud and Broca would have a word to say here in favour of their respective theories.

In further support of his views Van der Kolk quotes two cases, observed by Cruveilhier, in one of which the right corpus olivare had undergone grey degeneration, and in the other both these bodies were found as hard as cartilage.

Romberg mentions the case of a sailor, who, on being struck on the left side of the head by a loose rope, at once fell into a state of insensibility. After a quarter of an hour he recovered consciousness, but was found to have lost the use of the right half of the body, and to have become speechless. Three weeks afterwards the mobility of the extremities had been restored, and the tongue could be moved in every direction without difficulty, but the faculty of speech was arrested; and although perfectly conscious, it was only with the greatest effort that he was able to utter a few inarticulate sounds. Some blood was taken locally on several occasions by leeches applied behind the left ear, a combination of sulphate of magnesia and tartar emetic being administered at the same time; and in three weeks from the commencement of this treatment his speech returned, and he was completely restored.* He also mentions an interesting case of impairment of the speech, with partial paralysis of the left side, which after death was seen to depend upon a large tumour, seated in the right half of the pons Varolii, and extending posteriorly under the right olivary body.†

Dr. Bergmann, of Hildesheim, has written a masterly

* On the Nervous Diseases of Man.   Translated by Dr. Sieveking, p. 310.
† Ibid, p. 407.

treatise on loss of memory and of speech, illustrating it by a series of well recorded cases, to some of which I propose very briefly to refer.*

A ploughman, Wt., aged 40, of short stature, fell through the trap door of a garret upon the left side of the head. Much blood immediately flowed from the left ear and mouth, the bleeding from the ear continuing for two days. For four weeks he lay stunned and without power of recollection; he heard nothing, his speech was unintelligible, and his eyes were closed. When his consciousness was fully recovered, it was noticed that both eyes were turned towards the nose, (there was double convergent strabismus), the pupils were somewhat dilated and sluggish, there was intolerance of light and diplopia; his memory was observed to have suffered in a peculiar manner—the memory of *proper names and of substantives* was abolished, whilst that of *things and places* remained unimpaired; and he also had retained the power of correctly speaking and using *verbs*. He knew what he wished and ought to say, but could not connect the letters of substantives one with another. He knew exactly the place, the way, the streets, and their names, although he was quite unable to give utterance to these names. The same defect was noticed in reference to the furniture, and in fact to every other object. He was shown a penknife, a key, a looking glass, and he described their use by a periphrase. He said of the scissors which were shown him—it is what we cut with. On pointing to the windows he said, it is what we see through—what admits light.

* Einige Bemerkungen über Störungen des Gedächtniss und der Sprache, Allgemeine Zeitschrift für Psychiatrie, 1849, S. 657.

A man of large stature, strong constitution, and ruddy complexion, with knowing, lively, expressive eyes, for upwards of ten years had never spoken a single word, not even a yes or no, when alone or in company. He heard well, had a good memory, and a proper supply of ideas. He wrote a particularly firm and correct hand, and was never tired of putting his ideas and foolish fancies on paper. From these written effusions it was seen that his principal delusion was that he considered himself a great lord and potentate, who sent his decrees and decisions forth to the world. He was always accusing others, but in the most dignified language; and he commanded and gave his instructions after the manner of one learned in the law of the highest courts of appeal. It was evident that he had intelligence, but a perverted one; he heard and understood, as his written answers and other behaviour clearly showed. He was docile, he waited on the other patients like a brave nurse, and willingly employed himself with ordinary handiwork. During the many years that this man remained under observation, no means were left untried to ascertain whether he could be made to speak; but no fraud, no surprise, no sudden or sharp pain, no electric shock, no hot iron, no entreaty, no threat had ever succeeded in extracting from him even the slightest yes or no.

Dr. Bergmann, in commenting upon this singular case, and in endeavouring to reach the explanation of the physiological and pathological enigma involved in it, suggests two hypotheses: That there may have been a fixed idea, a fixed will, a caprice, an obstinate strong purpose, his physiognomy seeming to say—I remain still firm and true to myself, I will carry out my purpose, I will triumph, and I will not yield. Then on the other hand, if one considers that he was good-hearted and well-disposed, obliging and friendly, and that he was scarcely ever angry, notwithstanding all the opposition to his wishes, it would seem more probable that there was a real organic inner momentum *(inneres organisches Moment)*, some hidden impediment which produced loss of speech.

The only remaining case from this author to which I shall allude is that of Anna W., æt. 30, who up to the age of twenty was sound in mind and body, when a nervous fever laid the foundation of mental disturbance and chronic headache. After a time weakness of memory was noticed, and she became indifferent, unfeeling, and unsympathising. There was this peculiarity about the memory—that it was particularly weak and almost extinct in reference to subjects of recent date, whilst she could well remember the events of the earlier period of her illness. For upwards of two years she had never spoken a word, however much one roused her, although her manner gave unmistakable evidence that she could hear and understand what she heard. She had thoughts, conceptions, and ideas; there must then, says Dr. Bergmann, be an organic defect which rendered her unable to give vent to her thoughts by means of words or even by a sound.

I shall again have occasion to refer to Dr. Bergmann's highly philosophical treatise in another part of this essay.

Dr. Hasbach, of Geldern, has recorded the following case of *left hemiplegia with aphasia :*—A merchant, aged thirty-six, with a robust, thick-set body, who, from speculating in the funds, became in a short time very rich, was suddenly seized in the night after a hearty meal with apoplexy, resulting in complete paralysis of the left arm and leg, and loss of speech. After a month's treatment, the paralysis of the leg had so far subsided that he could walk slowly with the aid of a stick, the upper extremity remaining, however, entirely paralysed and deprived of sensation. With the exception of one single phrase, he did not recover the power of speech, the only words he could articulate being, "*gerechter Gott*," which he would repeat a hundred times each day. There was also this remarkable peculiarity, that although he could pronounce clearly and distinctly so difficult a phrase as gerechter Gott, he was quite unable to articulate separately the letters of which this expression was composed.[*]

Dr. W. Nasse, of Bonn, has written a valuable essay on defects of speech, in which he mentions the case of a man thirty years of age, who, after repeated attacks of apoplexy, was paralysed on one side of the body, retaining possession of his mental faculties. The movements of his tongue were unfettered, and he could make himself understood; in the middle of his sentences, however, he often applied wrong words, but immediately recognised his mistake, expressed concern for it, and would endeavour to extricate himself from his difficulty by gesture and periphrase. If the required word were named before him, he would repeat it with glib tongue, and could also write it down. After repeated attacks of cerebral congestion, the power of speech progressively diminished, and he gradually fell into a state of imbecility.

[*] Allgemeine Zeitschrift für Psychiatrie, 1852, S. 262.

Dr. Nasse, in his general remarks, calls attention to the fact that most frequently proper names and substantives, words which are first learnt in childhood, and which are in more general use, seem to disappear, whilst verbs and adjectives, which are acquired later, remain preserved. He also thinks the loss of the memory of words bears no relation to the condition of the muscular power *

Von Benedikt and Braunwart have an excellent and exhaustive paper on lesions of the faculty of speech, from which I shall only quote the following case of *aphasia from lead poisoning*, as reported by Heymann. †

Jacob Asthoiner, journeyman plasterer, aged sixteen, had suffered for many years from time to time, with lasting headache. Eventually, in the otherwise taciturn patient, were observed great vivacity and wantonness, and the ordinary symptoms of plumbism. A few days afterwards he ceased to answer any questions, and was unable to utter a syllable; there was also agraphia. A fortnight later his speech partially returned, and he spoke a few words very indistinctly, and would for many hours together cry out Va-ater, Mau-auter, and also Hu-unger with joyful, excited voice. This patient gradually but entirely recovered.

It will be observed that in some of the preceding cases, the subjects of them were lunatics or persons of weak mind; in my opinion, they are none the less valuable on that account; in fact, Broca's first two cases, the publication of which has given rise to so

---

* Allgemeine Zeitschrift für Psychiatrie, 1853, S. 525.
† Canstatts Jahresbericht, 1865; Dritter Band, S. 31.

much discussion and research throughout the scientific
world, were observed by that distinguished pathologist
in an institution devoted to the treatment of the various
forms of mental disease. Although aphasia is by no
means a very common symptom in the insane, I cannot
but think that the alienist physician possesses unusual
opportunities for contributing to the solution of what
still remains one of the most difficult questions in
cerebral pathology.

Amongst British authors the earliest observations
that have come under my notice are those of Crichton,
who, in his chapter on Memory, mentions several cases
bearing on the subject under consideration, from which
I have selected the following :—

An attorney, in his seventieth year, having indulged
in great venereal excesses, was suddenly seized with
great prostration of strength, giddiness, insensibility to
all the concerns of life, and every symptom of approach-
ing fatuity. When he wished to ask for anything, he
constantly made use of some inappropriate term;
instead of asking for a piece of bread he asked for his
boots, and if these were brought he knew they did not
correspond to the idea he had of the things he wanted,
and therefore he became angry, yet he would still
demand some of his boots or shoes, meaning bread.
If he wanted a tumbler, he would ask for a chamber
utensil, and if it happened to be the said chamber
utensil he wanted, he would ask for a tumbler, or a
dish. He evidently was conscious he used wrong
words, for when the proper expression was spoken by
another person, and he was asked if it was such a thing

he wanted, he always seemed aware of the mistake, and corrected himself by adopting the appropriate expression. This gentleman was cured of his complaint by large doses of valerian and other proper remedies.

Crichton also mentions instances of persons who suddenly found that they could not remember their own names, the most striking being that of an ambassador at St. Petersburgh, who, on calling at a house where he was not known by the servants, and wishing to give his name, could not remember it, and turning round to his companion said, with much earnestness, "For God's sake tell me who I am."

Baillie relates the history of a gentleman, aged fifty-six, who, after an attack of right hemiplegia, lost the recollection of the words of his own language, except a very few, "Yes," "No," "Mr. Reed," "Yesterday," which he employed on all occasions, and pronounced with the greatest distinctness, exhibiting none of that thickness in his pronunciation which is so common in paralytic patients; his countenance expressed a full share of understanding, and he seemed to comprehend all that was said to him. In the account of the necropsy, the brain and its membranes are described as perfectly natural in appearance, but the left vertebral artery was enlarged, and its coats had become opaque; there was considerable effusion into the lateral ventricles, which probably coincided with the occurrence of the coma which set in a few days previous to his death.*

Bright describes a case of dextral paralysis with aphasia, occurring in a man aged 63, who had a few

* Medical Transactions of the College of Physicians, Vol. iv.

years before married a woman much younger than
himself; he had also for several years been the subject
of an open ulcer in the leg, which had healed up six or
seven months before the paralytic seizure. After death
there was found softening of the middle and posterior
lobes of the left hemisphere, the anterior lobe being
unimpaired.   The vessels at the base of the brain,
particularly the carotid and its branches, were very
much ossified, and the mitral valve was converted into
an irregular bony mass.   There is a very beautiful
plate appended to the description of this case, from
which it would appear that the disease commenced in
the cortical portion.*

Dr. Copland, who has written *de omnibus rebus et
quibusdam aliis*, has, of course, not omitted to speak of
lesions of speech; our great medical lexicographer,
however, seems only to have viewed them as motor
defects, and not as due to the loss of an intellectual
faculty; and the only case which is given in detail in
his work on apoplexy, is clearly one of disease at the
origin of the lingual and glosso-pharyngeal nerves, and
not an instance of lesion of the faculty of articulate
language.†

Sir Thomas Watson relates a remarkable case of a
gentleman, who had a sudden fit of apoplexy, for which
he was freely bled, and who on the third day was
apparently quite recovered. On the fifth day, after a
long conversation, he suddenly lost the thread of his
discourse, became confused, and misappropriated words

* Reports of Medical Cases, Vol. ii., p. 177.
† Copland on Palsy and Apoplexy, p. 37.

—for instance, wishing to say "camphor," he called it "pamphlet." After a few days the right side of the body became paralysed, and he died at the expiration of a fortnight from the commencement of the attack. At the post mortem, an abscess was found at the upper part of the left hemisphere, in the centre of which was a small fibrous tough mass of dull red colour, the coagulum doubtless of blood effused at the period of the apoplectic seizure.*

Dr. Todd mentions several instances of hemiplegia with aphasia, the paralysis being, with one exception, always on the right side. In one case only the post mortem appearances are given, with Dr. Todd's usual attention to details. The hemiplegia was explained by disease of the central ganglia, but there was likewise considerable softening (colourless) of the white substance of the hemisphere, where were numerous small vessels in a state of fatty degeneration, and also an abundance of compound cells. The grey matter was not stated as being affected.† Dr. Todd's attention was evidently never given to the special consideration of speechlessness as a symptom of brain disease, and in one case, he says, "it was evident that very grave lesion had occurred, sufficient to inflict so severe a shock on the brain as to destroy the power of speech."

Dr. Forbes Winslow, in his remarkable chapter on the "Morbid Phenomena of Speech," has entered with considerable detail into the question of the cerebral localisation of that faculty, illustrating the subject by

* Practice of Physic, Vol. ii., p. 511.
† Clinical Lectures on Diseases of the Brain, p. 247.

allusion to a number of highly interesting cases, from which I have selected the following for brief allusion.*

A gentleman had an attack of apoplexy, consequent upon extravasation, the effects of a rupture of one of the cerebral vessels. He rallied, had a second attack, and again recovered. At the expiration of eighteen months a third attack ensued, when he became hemiplegic and entirely lost his speech, and died in two months, having never uttered a vocal sound. At the examination, a small patch of softened brain was found in the pons Varolii, surrounding a clot which had been deposited on that ganglion. The other portions of the cerebral mass were apparently in a healthy condition, with the exception of some of the vessels being closed by deposits of bony matter.

A patient suffering from cancer of the uterus, which completely prostrated her, was suddenly seized, in the middle of the night and without any known cause, with an almost complete dumbness, which only enabled her to say "yes, yes," to all questions, whether they were contradictory or not. She retained possession of her intelligence, for she was neither paralysed nor insane. If she was requested to write what she had to communicate, she traced an assemblage of letters on the paper to which no meaning could be attached.

A clergyman, whilst reading the Litany, became suddenly speechless, without losing his consciousness, and was obliged to leave the church. He continued in the same state for an hour, being perfectly sensible of everything that was going on about him, and was able to write on a piece of paper a request that a certain physician should be immediately summoned. Two

* On Obscure Diseases of the Brain, p. 497.

days after the loss of speech he was in a state of apoplectic coma, in which he died, no autopsy being permitted.

A gentleman, after many premonitory warnings, fell down in a fit, described as a combination of epilepsy and apoplexy, and for two days his life was in imminent danger; he, however, partially recovered, but with an inability to give anything like a clear expression to his wishes, what he said being quite unintelligible. He was able to pronounce words with great clearness, but they were sadly misplaced and transposed. By adopting the course of writing down what he said, and then re-arranging the words in their proper order, his family were able clearly to understand his wishes. This state of brain and impairment of speech continued with slight intermission for nearly a fortnight, accompanied by acute pain in the occipital region. Abstraction of blood by cupping was followed by a decided mitigation of the symptoms. Mercurial purgatives were administered, the head was shaved, and counter-irritation applied behind the ears. At the end of five days he was able to converse coherently for a few minutes, but if he continued in conversation beyond that time, he again began to jumble and misplace his words. Minute doses of bichloride of mercury, in combination with tincture of cinchona, were subsequently administered with the greatest benefit, and in the course of a few months he entirely recovered.

Dr. Winslow adds that in fifty-four cases he has detected after death a considerable amount of disease of the anterior lobes without being accompanied during life with any perceptible loss of speech. In one case of softening of the cerebellum, the principal symptom was

great perversion of the faculty of speech, without complete loss of power over this function, the anterior lobes
being free from all organic alteration.   In another case,
a large encysted abscess was discovered at the base of
the brain, which produced during life the most singularly remarkable modification of the faculty of speech,
the patient's misplacement of words being at times
most eccentric and grotesque, and the power of articulation seeming occasionally to be entirely lost.   In a
third case, a tumour of a malignant character was found
in the cerebellum, which produced complete loss of
speech.

The next observation to which I shall direct attention
is one of extreme interest from its exceptional character,
being a case of impairment of the faculty of articulate
language from *disease of the spinal cord*, reported by
Dr. Maty in the third volume of the London Medical
Observations and Inquiries.

The Count de L., aged 35, was overturned in his
coach from a high and steep bank; the accident was
followed by no head symptoms, and he soon recoverd
from the effects of a severe contusion of the left
shoulder, arm, and hand, and went through the fatigues
of a military campaign.   Six months afterwards, however, weakness of the left arm occurred, with difficulty
of articulating certain words.   Some months later the
difficulty in speaking and in moving the left arm
increased; the limb eventually became withered, and
he could scarcely utter a few words, and those only
monosyllables.   During all this time the Count continued able to read and write, and spent his time in the
most abstruse subjects, and up to the period of his

death, which occurred four years after the accident, he
preserved to the last the highest intellectual power.
The description of the autopsy is too minute to admit
of its being given here in detail; the medulla oblongata
was enlarged by one third, and more compact than
natural, and the spinal membranes were very tough.
The spinal marrow itself had acquired such a solidity
as to elude the pressure of the fingers, and to offer
the resistance of a callous body, this peculiarity being
most apparent in the cervical portion.

The following unique case of aphasia, resulting from
the rupture of a vessel within the orbit, was lately communicated to the Norwich Pathological Society by my
colleague, Dr. Copeman, who had extracted it from the
private notes of the late Mr. Norgate.

Sarah Hase, æt 29, a spare, slender woman, in good
general health and in the last stage of pregnancy, was
seized with an acute, lancinating pain in the left side of
the head and temple, extending deep into the orbit; the
eyelids became swollen, and she experienced a throbbing
and constant "boiling" just above the brow. At five
o'clock the following morning, with very little effort
and before the midwife could arrive, she was delivered
of a child. Soon afterwards the pain and distension
caused by pressure on the ocular globe from behind
became almost intolerable; and it now became quite
evident that a vessel of some size at the back of the
orbit had been ruptured. Leeches were now plentifully
applied around the part, followed by cold lotions. In
the evening of the same day, the eye was noticed to be
protruding and nearly immovable from pressure, and it
was now that for the first time Mr. Norgate noticed a

remarkable hesitation in answering questions, although she was perfectly conscious; she occasionally employed one word for another, mistook letters, and dropped syllables in articulating words. The next day the eyeball was more perfectly fixed, the agony was extreme, and although the cornea was then clear, the retina was amaurotic, and the iris quite insensible to light, vision of course being lost. She now confused her words so much as to be quite unintelligible to those around her; she tried to make it understood by signs that she wished to write, and in attempting to do so she invariably made use of parts of words. Omitting the daily details, suffice it to say that after scarification of the conjunctiva and other appropriate treatment, there was a little relaxation of pressure; the globe was less distended, and the power of expressing herself began to improve; in proportion as absorption proceeded, so the power of language increased, and in a few days she could articulate and converse as well as ever. This patient told Mr. Norgate afterwards that she comprehended everything that was said during the period in which she had been unable to express herself.

The above case is, I think, unique of its kind, although a somewhat similar one is quoted by Van der Kolk, from the "Gazette Médicale de Paris," of September 5th, 1857, where it is stated that in consequence of a wound, a bony splinter from the os frontis above the left eye compressed the anterior part of the hemisphere, subsequently causing loss of speech, which faculty was completely regained after the removal of the fragment by the trepan.

I would call attention to the fact that the inference to be drawn from these two cases is not in favour of

the theory of M. Broca, but rather favours the system
of Gall, who located the faculty of language in that
part of the anterior lobes which lies above the orbital
plates; for it was clearly this region that was the seat
of pressure in both cases, and not the neighbourhood of
the so-called Broca's region.

The next case I shall mention was also observed by a
Norwich pathologist—my colleague, Mr. Cadge, having
at a recent meeting of our Pathological Society, related
the following case of a cerebral tumour sufficiently large
to take the place of the left anterior lobe, speech continuing unaffected to the last.

C. D., æt. 50, was a strong stout man, remarkable
for his physical power and invariable good health, and
moderately temperate in his mode of life. Although
not an ill-tempered or violent man, he had a habit of
wrangling with, and abusing those in his employ; he
was addicted, in fact, to a kind of chronic vituperation,
which meant little, but sounded a good deal, for he had
a loud voice and a copious vocabulary. The first indication of his illness that attracted notice, was that
he ceased to upbraid, and became suspiciously good-
humoured and quiet; this change in his manner occurred
only six months before his death. The next symptom
was violent but intermitting headache; at first it was
almost confined to the back of the head, afterwards it
passed over to the forehead, but was never restricted to
one or other side of the head; he also had a constant
singing in the left ear. His sight soon became defective,
and about three months before death he became totally
blind, large retinal extravasation being observable by
the ophthalmoscope. As the sight failed, his mind and

faculties began to waver, and he became droll and
almost childish. At no period of his illness was there
any continued paralysis; on one occasion he staggered
and fell whilst walking, but quickly recovered. Other
than this, there was no loss of power or sensation; his
voice was clear and his articulation distinct. Six
months from the commencement of his illness he suddenly became apoplectic and comatose, and died in
twelve hours. Necropsy:—The cerebral membranes
were adherent; there was nothing like excessive congestion in any part, nor was there more than a little
excess of fluid either in the ventricles or at the base of
the brain. There was some trouble in peeling off the
membranes from the convolutions; this being as much
or more due to over softness of the latter than to unnatural adhesion; nothing like inflammation or active
congestion was present. Hidden in the left anterior
lobe of the brain, was a tumour of about the size of a
hen's egg; the tissue around it being considerably
softened, it was not easy to ascertain very precisely its
exact limits and relations. It seemed to occupy the
left lobe chiefly, encroaching slightly on the right
across the corpus callosum; behind it pressed on the
corpus striatum, and was visible in the anterior cornu
of the ventricle; in front it encroached upon the grey
matter of the convolutions, but did not reach the surface; below it rested on the root of the orbit and on the
olfactory nerve. The tumour itself was of softish consistency, not unlike tubercular matter; in some parts it
had almost a gelatinous aspect, and under the microscope
nothing was visible but a multitude of compound cells
and free nuclei, and a few large corpuscles, but no
fibrous structure whatever.

After stating that the inference was that the tumour was malignant, (its rapid development encouraging that view,) Mr. Cadge asks, why a tumour in the anterior lobe should cause blindness, as there was no pressure on, or inflammation around, the optic nerves, nor were the optic thalami or tract at all interfered with ? He also asks how it is that there was neither aphasia nor paralysis of the right side ? This last question of Mr. Cadge I shall endeavour to answer in a subsequent part of this essay, when analysing the mass of evidence I have collected with the view of testing the value of the different statements that have been made as to the seat of the faculty of speech.

Mr. Dunn, whose researches in physiological psychology are so well known, has published several very interesting cases of loss or impairment of speech, to one only of which I shall briefly refer.

A young girl, aged eighteen, accidentally fell into a river, from which she was extricated in a state of suspended animation ; prompt assistance being rendered, sensibility was restored, and she eventually recovered. Ten days afterwards she was seized with a fit, lay in a state of complete stupor for nearly four hours, on rallying from which, it was observed that she had lost the power of speech and hearing, and was also deprived of the senses of taste and smell, and for three months her only medium of communication with the external world were the senses of sight and touch. About three months afterwards, an incident occurred in the family which roused her sensibility and suddenly brought into play one of her suspended powers—the faculty of speech. Seeing her mother in a state of excessive agitation and

grief, she became excited herself, and in the emotional
paroxysm of the moment, she suddenly ejaculated,
"Wh—a—t's the mat—ter?" From this time she
began to articulate a few words, but she neither called
persons nor things by their right names. Nine months
later, under sudden and overwhelming emotional excitement, she fell into a state of insensibility of many
hours' duration, but which proved critical and sanatory,
for she awoke in possession of her natural faculties and
former knowledge; her speech was restored, but she
had not the slightest recollection of anything that had
taken place during the interval of the twelve months
that her faculties had been suspended.

Beyond all doubt the observer who has done the
most in this country to elucidate the subject of cerebral
loss of speech, is Dr. Hughlings Jackson, who, in the
London Hospital Reports for 1864, has given the
details of thirty-four cases of hemiplegia with loss of
speech. Of these cases, the paralysis was observed
thirty-one times on the right side and three times on
the left; the heart was more or less affected in twenty
instances (valvular disease existing in thirteen cases);
in four cases there was loss or defect of smell. I much
regret that want of space will not allow me to dwell on
this most interesting communication; there are, however, two cases in this collection to which I must briefly
allude. One is a case of *aphasia with left hemiplegia*
occurring suddenly in a gentleman 64 years of age,
who fourteen years before had received a very severe
blow in the right occipital region, which had left him
ever afterwards deprived of the power of smell and
taste. In the other case the patient, although con-

tinuing aphasic, had recovered the power to *swear;*
which Dr. Jackson explains on the principle, that
ejaculatory expressions are prompted by the emotions
and not by the will; he also considers that oaths and
similar interjectional expressions are not parts of speech
in the broad sense in which the words that form them
are, when used to convey intellectual propositions.

The Medical Journals of the last few years contain a
variety of interesting cases, to the salient points of
which only a passing allusion can be made.

In the "Medical Times" of July 9th, 1864, a case is
recorded of a man aged twenty-one who was admitted
into the Middlesex Hospital, under Dr. Stewart, with
left hemiplegia without loss of speech, the attack having
been preceded by choreic movements of the left arm
and leg. A week later, he was suddenly seized with
paralysis of the *right* side, with loss of speech, consciousness however being retained. After death both
middle cerebral arteries were filled with fibrinous plugs
and semi-coagulated blood; at each end of the Sylvian
fissure was a mass of diffluent brain substance, of about
the size of a walnut.

In the "British Medical Journal" for Dec. 14, 1867,
Dr. Bastian reports a case of right hemiplegia with
aphasia, where after death the arteries at the base of
the brain were all notably diseased and contained large
white calcified patches at intervals; the left hemisphere
showed very many patches of red softening, which were
almost always strictly confined to the grey matter of
the convolutions, the principal patches of softening
being met with in the *third or inferior frontal convolution .*

in a portion of the adjacent ascending parietal,* near
its commencement, and in the superior frontal. The
great mass of the white matter of the hemisphere
appeared healthy and of normal consistence, as also the
central ganglia, pons, and medulla. The heart was
large, weighing eighteen ounces; the aortic valves and
a portion of the great tongue of the mitral, showed a
very early atheromatous change.

One of the most recent observations that has fallen
under my notice is that recorded by Dr. Simpson, in
the "Medical Times" of Dec. 21, 1867, as a case of
"*Extensive Lesion of the left inferior frontal convolution
of the cerebrum without aphasia.*" W. M., æt. 62, was
admitted into the Gloucester County Asylum, in
February, 1857, and had been subject to epilepsy from
his early youth; he never had an apoplectic attack as
far as could be ascertained, nor had he at any time
suffered from loss of speech. During the ten years he
was under observation in the asylum, he had no brain
symptoms beyond those ordinarily associated with
epilepsy, no paralysis, and no impairment of speech.
He died in November, 1867, of bronchitis. Autopsy:—
Calvarium thick and heavy; cranium unsymmetrical,
being elongated in the left oblique diameter. Dura
mater non-adherent and healthy; arachnoid opaque
throughout, but more particularly on the upper parts of
both hemispheres; pia mater normal. The grey matter
was somewhat atrophied, of firm consistence, but paler
than normal; white matter also atrophied, and the
interspaces and ventricles filled with serum. Both
orbital divisions of the frontal lobes were indented, from
undue prominence of the upper walls of the orbits. On

* I presume Dr. Bastian means the posterior or ascending frontal.

the left side, and implicating the *posterior part of the third or inferior frontal convolution*, a large depression existed which appeared to be the remains of an apoplectic clot; it was of irregular shape, about an inch and three-quarters in its antero-posterior, and an inch and a half in its transverse diameters; extending internally to within five lines of the olfactory bulb, and in front to within an inch of the anterior margin of the hemisphere; it was deepest in the centre, where it measured half an inch from the general line of surface. The brain tissue was stained of a brownish-yellow colour, and there was considerable puckering, with induration round the margins of the depression. Microscopical examination showed distinct feathery crystals of hæmatoidin. The cortical substance was greatly thinned, being reduced to a mere line in the centre of the depression; the island of Reil appeared healthy, and the other parts of the brain presented no great deviation from the normal standard; the cerebral arteries were slightly atheromatous. Weight of encephalon, 42½ oz.

These three cases, the leading features only of which I have just described, are of extreme interest from the circumstance that in all of them the clinical history is completed by a minute and well-recorded description of the post-mortem appearances. The first case is remarkable from the fact that the patient possessed the power of speech in its perfect integrity whilst the paralysis was confined to the *left* side; but, having to a great extent recovered from this first attack, a sudden invasion of *dextral* paralysis was immediately followed by loss of speech. The second case, that of Dr. Bastian, will be claimed by M. Broca and his advocates in support of their theory as to the localisation of speech, for there is a high probability that the diseased action may have commenced in the third or inferior frontal convolution and its neighbourhood, as the greatest amount of softening was observed in this region; another interesting feature in the case was the existence of complete hemiplegia with only disease of the convolutional grey matter to account for it. This remarkable communication, which is written in Dr. Bastian's usual clear and lucid style, is well worthy of a careful study, being pregnant with original thought and the results of philosophical research. The case of Dr. Simpson is unique, and cannot be dismissed without a word of comment. Here there was disease of the posterior part of the third frontal convolution, (the exact region of Broca,) without any impairment of speech. I have already mentioned cases of aphasia where the frontal convolutions were all described as healthy, and I shall have others to record, which have occurred under my own immediate observation; but hitherto we have had no example of the converse condition, that is, *disease of the third frontal convolution without lesion of speech*, and it has even been stated that there is no case on record in which positive disease of this precise spot existed with integrity of speech.

The researches of our northern neighbours, the Professors of the " *Modern Athens*," must be considered as most valuable contributions to the literature of the subject we are now discussing.

Abercrombie, whose work on cerebral disease is perhaps more quoted than that of any other British author of the past generation, has recorded numerous cases of cerebral loss of speech, of which I can only briefly allude to the following, which are in direct opposition to the recent theories as to the seat of the faculty of articulate language.

A man, aged fifty, who had been for some time subject to cough and bloody expectoration, was seized with frontal headache and some confusion of thought, which appeared chiefly in a tendency to misapply words; he soon lost the sight of the right eye, his speech became indistinct, and, after some time, inarticulate; and he died in two months from the commencement of the cerebral symptoms. At the autopsy there was found, at the *posterior* part of the left hemisphere, a soft and vascular cyst, containing about two ounces of a thick, colourless fluid, coagulable by heat, and exactly resembling the albumen of an egg; the cerebral substance around the cyst was softened, the brain in other respects being healthy.

A man, aged sixty, after some premonitory symptoms, was suddenly seized with *left hemiplegia and inarticulate speech*, his intelligence, however, being unimpaired. At the end of a month he was suddenly seized with perfect loss of speech, which was followed in a few hours by coma, from which he did not recover. The substance of the brain was found healthy, except at the outer part of the right hemisphere, where there was a considerable portion in a state of complete ramollissement. The pia mater on the upper part of both hemispheres appeared thickened, and was remarkably vascular; there was considerable subarachnoid effusion, and both lateral ventricles were distended with fluid.

The same author mentions the case of a child, four

E

years and a half old, whose articulation had been for
many months very imperfect, and at whose autopsy the
corpora olivaria, the crus cerebelli, and the tubercula
mammillaria were found in a state of cartilaginous
hardness; other parts being sound.*

In the report of the Edinburgh Asylum for 1866,
Dr. Skae speaks of a case of right hemiplegia where the
patient had lost the power of all articulate speech, except the words "aye, aye," and at whose autopsy, an
effusion of blood was found in the *left posterior lobe of
the brain.*

Dr. Sanders and Dr. Scoresby Jackson have each
recorded a case with autopsy, more or less corroborative
of Broca's theory.

The subject of Dr. Sanders' case was a woman aged
43, who was admitted into the Royal Infirmary at
Edinburgh, on November 16th, 1865, with incomplete
paralysis of the right side, defective speech, and loss of
the memory of words. Without following Dr. Sanders
in his detailed account of the clinical history of this
case, suffice it to say, that two days after admission the
patient complained of pain in the *left* leg, with impaired motion and anæsthesia; signs of obstruction of
the left femoral artery shewed themselves, and gangrene
of the corresponding limb occurred, from the effects of
which she died about two months from the date of her
admission. Autopsy :—The right hemisphere presented
no lesion. On carefully examining the left hemisphere,
the posterior part of the inferior left frontal convolution,
where it forms the anterior margin of the fissure of
Sylvius, together with a small portion of the adjoining

* On Diseases of the Brain and Spinal Cord, pp. 176, 273, 431.

orbital convolution, was observed to be collapsed, and depressed below the natural level. The flattened and depressed portions felt soft and fluctuating to the touch, and on cutting into the softened part, the grey matter was found to be thinned off from within, and the white cerebral substance was completely softened and eroded, presenting an appearance like dirty cream. The softening extended inwards to the immediate neighbourhood of the corpus striatum, without, however, involving it. The other convolutions of the anterior lobe were not affected, but there existed a separate softening near the posterior extremity of the fissure of Sylvius. The corpora olivaria were normal, and there was no other lesion of the encephalon. There was no embolism in the cerebral arteries, but there was a little thickening in the wall of the artery of the left Sylvian fissure.*

In Dr. Scoresby Jackson's case, the subject of it, James A., 48 years of age, was thrown from a van and received a wound on the left temple. This accident did not prevent him from working, but he ever afterwards complained of a pain in the head; and two months after the injury, he was suddenly seized with right hemiplegia and aphasia, and died seven weeks later. Autopsy:—The heart was of natural size, and on the mitral valve were numerous vegetations, and loose fibrinous masses. The vessels at the base of the brain were atheromatous at several points, and there was

* Since the above lines were written, I have been favoured with a private communication from Dr. Sanders, in which he tells me that his later dissections tend to show that in speech palsy it is the island of Reil that is at fault, rather than Broca's convolution. For the details of cases published by Dr. Sanders in support of this view, see Lancet for June 16th, 1866, and Edinburgh Medical Journal for August, 1866.

embolism in some of the branches of the left middle
cerebral artery. There was softening of a considerable
portion of the left hemisphere, being most advanced in
the island of Reil and in the posterior part of the third
frontal convolution, the anterior end of the same gyrus
not being involved.*

Dr. Gairdner, of Glasgow, has published an extremely interesting case of epileptic (?) seizure, followed
by a speechless and somewhat cataleptic state, without
coma or evident paralysis. There was recovery of the
intelligence to a considerable extent, but with continued
aphasia, death ensuing in ten weeks during an epileptic
paroxysm. This patient, although unable to express
himself in writing, was able to copy handwriting set
before him with tolerable accuracy. The necropsy,
which was made with great care, revealed no cerebral
lesion whatever beyond general and diffused congestion
of the vessels of the pia mater, the smaller ones of which
were surrounded with slight granular deposit.†

Dr. Robertson, of Glasgow, after giving a most interesting account of three typical cases observed by
himself, gives the following summary of the views he
entertains as to the cause of aphasia:—"There is a
lesion usually in the left hemisphere of the brain, of
efferent fibres passing between the convolutions and the
great co-ordinating centres, probably at some point of
a line extending from the external frontal convolution
to the corpus striatum, so that voluntary motor impulses for the articulation of language cannot be trans-

* Edinburgh Medical Journal, February, 1867.
† Glasgow Medical Journal, May, 1866.

mitted. The essential morbid change is, therefore, *motor*, and not *mental*."*

Medical science is indebted to the physicians of the *"sister island"* for much valuable information communicated by them in reference to cerebral loss of speech.

In the *Dublin Quarterly Journal* for February, 1851, Graves has recorded a most singular instance of amnesic aphasia, limited to substantives and proper names. The subject of it was a Wicklow farmer, fifty years of age, who, after an attack of hemiplegia, was affected with an incapacity to employ nouns and proper names, he being able in other respects to express himself well. This defect was accompanied by the following singular peculiarity: that he perfectly recollected the *initial letter* of every substantive or proper name for which he had occasion in his conversation, though he could not recall to his memory the word itself. He consequently made for himself a little pocket dictionary of the words in most general use, including the proper names of his children, servants, and acquaintances, and during a conversation he would look in his dictionary till he found the word he wanted, keeping his finger and eye fixed on the word until he had finished the sentence, but the moment the book was closed, the word passed out of his memory and could not be recalled, although he recollected its initial, and could refer to it again in his dictionary when necessary. The learned Dublin professor, in his clinical lectures, has recorded two most interesting cases, where loss of speech was at first the

* The Pathology of Aphasia. Journal of Mental Science, Jan., 1867.

only morbid symptom, but he does not dwell on the pathology of this singular affection ; and, strange to say, although the cases recorded are typical instances of aphasia, he seems to imply that in loss of speech the defect may lie in the glottis rather than be the result of cerebral lesion !*

In the same journal for February, 1865, is a valuable paper by Dr. Banks, in which he mentions the following very curious case :—

A gentleman, now aged 54, was eight years since attacked with paralysis of the right side and aphasia. At first the loss of speech was complete, but after twelve days he could say a few words. Before his attack he was a ripe scholar, and had taken much pleasure in reading the best classical authors ; but when his stock of words had increased so as to enable him to converse a little on ordinary subjects, it was observed that his memory had quite failed him with respect to Greek and Latin. For six years he continued without improving to any considerable extent, but still he was gradually acquiring new words. For the next two years his progress was more rapid ; he laboured hard, and almost learned over again all that he had forgotten, so as to be able to read his old favourite classical authors once more. The accomplished Trinity College Professor adduces this case to prove that, even in aphasia with paralysis, the mind may remain unclouded, and the power of speech, even after years, may be re-established.

At the annual meeting of the British Medical Association held at Dublin last August, I had the pleasure of reading a paper on the "Localisation of the

* Clinical Medicine, p. 433.

Faculty of Speech," after which an interesting discussion took place, in which Professor Gairdner, Drs. Lyons, Hayden, Lalor, Gibson, &c., took a part; and some extraordinary cases of the sudden loss of speech, and of the intellectual results that followed, were mentioned.

During my visit to Dublin, Dr. Lyons kindly called my attention at the Hardwicke Hospital to a case of aphasia occurring as a complication of cerebro-spinal arachnitis.

The subject of it, John Oyden, a delicate boy, aged eleven years, was admitted into the hospital on May 30th, being reported three days ill. His symptoms were those of well marked cerebro-spinal arachnitis, of pure type, and intense degree. The face was flushed; the pupils were dilated; and the patient complained of much acute pain in the head and back of the neck, which extended down the spine for a considerable distance. On June 3rd, the usual eruption made its appearance. On June 25th the patient became affected with aphasia, the right side being at the same time paralysed. He remained in this state for many days; the only words he was able to utter were "day, day," which was his answer to all inquiries. In the beginning of July he rallied a good deal and regained the power of speech, but on August 27th he again became the subject of aphasia, in which state he died.*

Dr. Popham, of Cork, in a very elaborate paper in

---

* The above very meagre report of this remarkable case is taken from the British Medical Journal of September 28th, 1867 ; it is to be hoped, however, that Dr. Lyons will eventually favour us with a detailed account of this most interesting and exceptional case.

the *Dublin Quarterly Journal*, mentions the following case, which he says bears on M. Broca's views.

Mary Murphy, aged sixty, was admitted to the Union Hospital with right hemiplegia and impaired speech. The memory of words was very defective, and the articulation confused; for "thank you, Sir," she said "fancy sell," and being asked what her husband, a pedlar, sold, she replied "procties and pudding pans," which Dr. Popham found out meant "brooches and bosom pins." She eventually died of pneumonia, when the following appearances were observed at the post-mortem examination:—The heart was covered with fat, the mitral orifice was narrow, its margins ossified, and there were some vegetations on the auricular surface. There was considerable effusion under the arachnoid membrane. On careful examination of the left hemisphere, the convolution of Broca was softer in consistence than the neighbouring parts, and the remains of an apoplectic cyst, of the size of an almond, and empty, was situated close to the anterior third of the corpus striatum, and running parallel to its course.

I now arrive at the consideration of the labours of our American cousins, beginning with Dr. S. Jackson, of Pennsylvania, who records the following curious case.

The Rev. Mr. ——, æt. 48, endowed with intellectual powers of a high order, of a sanguine temperament, with latterly a strong tendency to obesity, having exposed himself to the influence of the night air, received a check to the cutaneous perspiration. The next morning he awoke with a headache, and when a friend went into his room to inquire after his health, he was surprised to find Mr. R—— could not answer his questions. Dr. Jackson having been summoned, found the patient in full possession of his senses, but incapable of uttering a word; the tongue was not paralysed, but could be moved in every direction; all questions were perfectly comprehended and answered by signs, and it could be plainly seen by the smile on the countenance, after many ineffectual attempts to express his ideas, that he was himself surprised, and somewhat amused at his peculiar situation. The face was flushed, the pulse full and somewhat slow, and to the inquiries if he suffered pain in the head, he pointed to his forehead as its seat. When furnished with pen and paper, he attempted to convey his meaning, but he could not recall words, and only wrote an unintelligible phrase, "Didoes doe the doe." Forty ounces of blood were drawn from the arm, and before the operation was completed speech was restored, though a difficulty continued as to the names of things, which could not be recalled. The loss of speech appearing to recur in fifteen minutes, ten ounces more blood were abstracted, and sinapisms supplied to the arms and thighs alternately. These means were speedily effectual, and no further return of the affection took place.

Dr. Jackson, in analysing this case, calls attention to the following facts. Firstly, sudden suppression of the cutaneous transpiration, succeeded by cerebral irritation and determination of blood to the brain: secondly, frontal pain immediately over the eye: thirdly, perfect integrity of the sensations and voluntary movements: fourthly, the general operations of the intellect undisturbed; ideas formed, combined, and compared; those of events, of time, recalled without difficulty: fifthly, loss of language or of the faculty of conveying ideas by words though not by signs; this defect not being confined to spoken language, but also extending to written language.*

Dr. Hun, of Albany, mentions the case of a blacksmith, æt. 35, who, before the present attack, could read and write with facility, but who had been labouring for several years under a disease of the heart. After a long walk in the sun, he was seized in the evening with symptoms of cerebral congestion, remaining in a state of stupor for several days. After a few days he began to recover from this condition, and understood what was said, but it was observed that he had great difficulty in expressing himself in words, and for the most part could only make his wants known by signs. There was no paralysis of the tongue, which he could move in all directions. He knew the meaning of words spoken before him, but could not recall those needed to express himself, nor could he repeat words when he heard them pronounced; he was conscious of the difficulty under which he was labouring, and seemed surprised and distressed at it. If Dr. Hun pronounced the word he needed, he seemed pleased, and would say, "Yes, that is it," but was unable to repeat the words after him. After fruitless attempts to repeat a word, Dr. Hun wrote it for him; and then he would begin to spell it letter by letter, and after a few trials, was able to pronounce it; if the writing were now taken from him, he could no longer pronounce the word; but after long study of the written word, and frequent repetition, he

* American Journal of Medical Sciences, February, 1829, p. 272.

would learn it so as to retain it and afterwards use it. He kept a slate, on which the words he required most were written, and to this he referred when he wished to express himself. He gradually learned these words and extended his vocabulary, so that after a time, he was able to dispense with his slate. He could read tolerably well from a printed book, but hesitated about some words; when he was unable to pronounce a word, he was also unable to write it until he had seen it written; and then he could learn to write as he learned to pronounce, by repeated trials. At the end of six months, by continually learning new words, he could make himself understood pretty well, often, however, employing circumlocution, when he could not recall the proper word, somewhat as if he were speaking a foreign language, imperfectly learned.

Dr. Hun infers, from what precedes, that there is a portion of the brain connected with language or the memory of words, as distinct from the memory of things and events; and that there is another portion on which depends the co-ordination of the movements of articulation. It will be observed that in the above case, the impression made on the acoustic nerve was not sufficient for rendering the articulation of the word possible, but that it was necessary that an impression should be made upon the optic nerve. Dr. Hun asks whether this can be explained by the supposition of a more intimate connection between vision and articulation, or by the fact that the impression on the acoustic nerve is transient, whilst that on the optic is more permanent.*

* American Journal of Insanity, April, 1851.

One of the most important American contributions to the literature of aphasia is that of Dr. Wilbur, the Superintendent of the State Asylum for Idiots, at Syracuse, N. Y., who has written an extremely interesting pamphlet, in which he treats the aphasic question, as illustrated by his own experience amongst idiots.

Of the 443 idiots he has had under his care, 121 were entirely mute—could not or did not utter a single word; 64 could say only a word or two; in 163 there was imperfect speech; and 95 are described in the register as able to speak. In these last cases, he adds, the ability to speak was commensurate, in some degree, with the intelligence; but, in a large proportion of them, there was great backwardness in learning to speak.

A large proportion, perhaps seventy-five per cent, of Dr. Wilbur's cases were congenital; the remainder had their faculties impaired by disease in infancy or early childhood. In these latter, when there was loss of speech, it occurred in some instances gradually, but more commonly instantly. He adds that intelligence, and speech or expression, have certainly not always gone with an equal step.

Dr. Wilbur gives the clinical history of his patients, with special reference to their loquelar defect; it is, however, much to be regretted that in no instance is the case completed by a post-mortem examination. I have selected the following case from Dr. Wilbur's collection, as tending to illustrate how much may be done towards partially developing speech in the idiot:—

A boy, eight years old, good looking and well formed, came under observation, idiocy having supervened in infancy. He looked intelligent, was very gentle and obedient; he understood any simple language addressed to him, or spoken in his hearing; he could repeat the sentences he heard, or the question spoken, but could originate nothing in the form of speech, under any circumstances. The control over his vocal organs was complete; he spoke quite distinctly, and with appropriate emphasis. He soon began to learn rapidly the exercises given to him, but the power or disposition to originate speech, even within the range of his wants or his affections was wanting. The failure in the power of speech seemed to be in the absence of the proper volition. In this case, the defect was overcome at last, through reading exercises, and eventually the boy could speak spontaneously.*

It may be said that imperfection of speech in the idiot is so intimately connected with a general want of intelligence, that it bears but little analogy to loss of speech as occurring in individuals of full intellectual capacity. Whilst, to some extent admitting this, when I consider Dr. Wilbur's great success in developing the power of expression in the idiot, I cannot but think that if other physicians with similar opportunities to his, would follow his example and place on record their own experience, a lasting benefit would be rendered to the cause of psychological science, and the solution of the particular question we are now discussing would be materially aided.

Dr. Austin Flint, in giving an account of six cases which had fallen under his observation, expresses his strong dissent from the doctrine of the localisation of the faculty of speech in the left hemisphere, and he thinks that anatomical researches may show why lesion of speech is a more constant accompaniment of dextral than of sinistral paralysis.

* On Aphasia, p. 23.

One of the latest communications that have come under my notice is a paper by Dr. Seguin, in which he gives a report of fifty cases of aphasia that have been observed at the New York Hospital. This essay contains much interesting matter, but the description of the cases is so meagre, as to render the collection conparatively useless for statistical purposes.*

Having in the preceding pages endeavoured to give a brief sketch of the labours of the principal authors in various parts of the world who have written on the subject of loss or impairment of the faculty of articulate language, I shall, in the next number, give the results of my own personal experience, as embodied in a series of important cases which have fallen under my own immediate observation.

* American Quarterly Journal of Psychological Medicine, Jan., 1868.

PART III.

HAVING in the preceding pages endeavoured critically to review the question of the localisation of the faculty of speech, as illustrated by the labours of the French, Dutch, and German pathologists, as well as by those of the different branches of the Anglo-Saxon race, I now proceed to place on record a certain number of cases which have been observed by myself, and in several of which the clinical history was completed by a careful *post-mortem* examination.

In some instances it may be thought that I have described the clinical history with too much minuteness, and with a fastidious attention to apparently unimportant details; but the question we are now considering is involved in so much obscurity, that it seems to me that it is only by carefully studying the various phases of cases which we have an opportunity of closely watching, that we can hope to contribute anything towards the solution of one of the most complex questions in cerebral pathology—a question about which so much has lately been written, and about which it seems to me so little is at present really known.

It will be observed that in several of the following cases I have given the volumetric analysis of the principal solid ingredients of the urine. This, to some persons, may seem a work of supererogation; to those I would say that the diagnosis of cerebral disease is involved in so much obscurity, that the serious and conscientious observer is bound to avail himself of every collateral aid within his reach; and it cannot be otherwise than useful, systematically to calculate the amount of phosphorus and other constant or occasional solid ingredients of nervous tissue which are daily eliminated from the system.

The following cases present various forms of the affection, from the uncomplicated pure form of aphasia—where there is simply abolition or suspension of speech without any paralytic or other morbid symptom—to the partial or even occasional impairment of that faculty; and here I would remark that in making investigations with the view of elucidating any obscure symptom or disease, the common error into which many observers fall, is to confine their attention to the consideration of typical cases only—cases where the symptom or disease is well marked and defined; whereas, as much or more information may sometimes be gained from the careful study of exceptional cases, and of cases where the particular symptom or disease is only slightly marked.

Impressed with these views, I have for some time past made careful notes of all cases that have fallen under my observation, where the faculty of articulate language was affected in any way or degree, however slight, deeming it quite as useful to study cases where the lesion of speech is a mere epiphenomenon, as where it forms the principal or the sole morbid symptom.

APHASIA OF THE ATAXIC FORM, OCCURRING AS THE EARLIEST MORBID SYMPTOM: SOME MONTHS LATER VERBAL AMNESIA: EPILEPTIFORM CONVULSIONS: ULTIMATELY GENERAL PARALYSIS.

William Sainty, a waterman, aged fifty-one, was admitted under my care into the Norfolk and Norwich Hospital, April 1st, 1865, with the following antecedent history:—He had always lived a temperate and steady life, had never contracted syphilis, nor suffered from any rheumatic affection—in fact, he 'had always enjoyed excellent health quite up to the period of the present attack, which was not preceded by any premonitory symptoms of brain or nervous disorder. On the 9th of December, 1864, after unloading his vessel, in which he had conveyed a cargo of goods from Norwich to Yarmouth, a distance of thirty miles, he went into a tavern with the intention of asking for some beer, when, to his astonishment and concern, he found he could not speak—the power of articulation was suddenly and completely suspended. Nothing odd or peculiar had been observed in his manner, and he had only a few hours previously called at a merchant's office and arranged about a fresh cargo, when his aptitude for business was in no wise impaired. · The loss of speech then was sudden, and was clearly unaccompanied by any other paralytic symptom, for although speechless, he, on the same evening, removed his vessel from one point of the river to another, and on the following day loaded it with a fresh cargo, after which, unaccompanied by any of his friends or comrades, he took the train to Norwich, and on his arrival walked from the railway station to his own home, a distance of a mile. His friends, alarmed at finding that his vocabulary was limited to the words "Oh! dear! oh! dear!" sent for a surgeon, under whose care he continued till a few days before he came to the hospital. I have not been able to procure any very accurate information as to the precise time during which the abolition of speech was complete; it would seem, however, that after three days he

F

could say a few words, but that it was not till the expiration of
a fortnight that there was any marked improvement; after this
period, the progress towards the partial recovery of his speech
seems to have been gradual. Sometime in February, he experienced a slight abnormal nervous symptom, characterised
by numbness in one of the fingers of the right hand. A month
later he had a kind of fit, falling down, and remaining for a
few minutes unconscious.

Symptoms on admission.—His condition is that of a healthy
looking man, with a remarkably intelligent countenance, looking
me straight in the face when addressed, and evidently understanding all that is said; but although his ideas seem to arise
in great number in his brain, and there is no want of sequence
in his thoughts, he is unable to give expression to those ideas
by articulate language, except in a very imperfect manner.
There is, also, partial agraphia, for although just able to form
one or two words, he cannot write a sentence, he being able to
write fluently and well before the present attack. He has the
proper use of all his limbs, which are free from the slightest
abnormal sensation. Deglutition is unaffected. The tongue
is protruded straight, and he can execute all the different movements appertaining to that organ. The only feature to notice
in the tongue is, that the right half is slightly raised above the
level of the left half, and is more flabby, and also that when told
to protrude the tongue, he keeps it out a long time, as if from
a defect of memory, probably not remembering what he had
done. There is no abnormal sensation about the head, and
the organs of special sense are unimpaired. He is very
cheerful, and does not weep from emotional causes, like
persons with ordinary paralysis; nor has he that distressed
countenance usually observed in the subjects of grave cerebral
disorder. The heart's action is feeble, with occasional inter-
mittence, but no evidence of valvular disease. Pulse, 72.
Urine, sp. gr. 1020, freely acid; no albumen, and a volumetric
analysis of the principal solid ingredients gave the following
result:—

Chlorides	-	-	- 10.5 parts per 1000
Urea	-	-	- 26 ,, ,,
Phosphoric acid (in combination)	1.5	,,	,,

So long a time having elapsed since the attack which had

produced the impairment of speech, I felt that but little could be done in the way of treatment. I prescribed for him small doses of the phosphates of iron and zinc, with dilute phosphoric acid, and under this treatment, together with a careful attention to diet, he slightly improved, the improvement being, however, more marked in his power of writing than in speaking. Discharged June 3rd.

Shortly after his discharge he resumed his work as a waterman, when no untoward symptom occurred till January, 1866, when, after a morning's work, as he was going into his cabin to prepare for dinner, he fell to the ground quite unconscious, and came to himself in about a quarter of an hour; but his speech for some hours was more embarrassed than usual; there was, however, no paralysis on recovery, for he resumed his work the same day. At the end of February (a month later) he again fell in his cabin, frothed at the mouth, was livid in the face, and remained unconscious half an hour; on recovery, there was increased embarrassment of speech for some hours, but before night he was as usual. There seems to have been no convulsive movements on either of these two occasions. After the above date he had a similar fit every few weeks.

Re-admitted January 12th, 1867.—He seems still in possession of all his intelligence, has no paralysis, nor even diminution of motor power. He understands all that is said, but is affected with an incapacity to employ substantives, having lost the memory of words as far as that part of speech is concerned, and he will make use of a periphrase to avoid using the substantive required. If asked to fetch an object he will bring the right, but if he wants anybody else to fetch or give him anything, he more commonly asks for the wrong thing first, afterwards correcting himself, showing that he understands perfectly what he wants. If shown anything he will say that he knows what it is, but cannot say it. On being shown a purse, and being asked what it was, he answered, "I can't say the word; I know what it is; it is to put money in." Is it a knife? No. An umbrella? No. A purse? Yes. I showed him a poker. What is it? I know, but cannot say the word. What is its use? To make up the fire. Is it a walking stick? No. Is it a broom? No. Is it a poker? Yes, he said, instantly, with a smile evincing complete understanding of the question, and joy at the certainty that he had answered it right.

March 30th.—The house surgeon was called to him to-day, and found him stretched on the floor, twitching convulsively, with turgid face, gnashing of the teeth, foaming at the mouth, eyes open and rolling, pupils dilated and insensible to light, breathing stertorous, skin cold and clammy. These symptoms continued for fifteen minutes, when violent jerking of the left leg and thigh occurred, the convulsive efforts ceased, and he gradually recovered his senses; there was no paralysis.

March 31st.—The patient had a sound sleep after the fit of yesterday, and to-day is as usual.

On showing him a tumbler glass he shakes his head, and says it is for beer, but cannot remember its name; he knows it is not called a basin, a mug, or a jug, and recognises the word glass directly it is named; but the next minute he has forgotten it, and cannot repeat it. He was also shown a warming pan, about which he became quite angry from his inability to remember its name; he, however, showed his interrogators what it was used for, with great despatch, and recognised its name the moment it was casually mentioned.

April 24th.—Suddenly taken speechless, with loss of motor power in the lower limbs, the upper extremities being unaffected. The fit was evidently entirely different from any other he has had; there were no epileptiform convulsions, simply faintness, speechlessness, and paraplegia. The pupils were equal and active; he appeared conscious of all that was going on around him, and as soon as he was put to bed he uttered confused sounds, but could not articulate.

25th.—The motor power in the lower limbs has partially returned; in fact, there is no actual paralysis this morning, there is simply want of co-ordinating power of the lower limbs; he can walk very imperfectly, supported by two persons, but cannot stand alone.

May 2nd.—I was summoned to him to-day, and found him in an epileptic fit, perfectly unconscious, pupils both contracted and immoveable, foaming at the mouth, with convulsions, which were confined to the right arm and leg and right side of the face; the right orbicularis palpebrarum was contracting violently; the left side of the body seemed unaffected; the convulsions soon affected both sides, the left, however, to a much less extent. Five grains of calomel to be put upon the tongue, and a turpentine injection to be administered.

3rd.—He is still quite unconscious—in fact, in a state of

epileptic coma; pupils still contracted and immoveable, and there is imperfect right hemiplegia, without loss of sensation.

4th.—The hemiplegia has passed off, there being only a little loss power in the arm; consciousness is returning.

5th.—Pupils still contracted and insensible to light; he has recovered consciousness, and has evidently now the use of all his limbs. He cannot stand alone, but he walked some yards this morning, with the assistance of two persons. He put his hand to his forehead as if in pain, and he is becoming restless, and requires a person constantly by his side to keep him in his bed.

In a few days he had gradually recovered the power to stand and even walk alone a few steps; he continued, however, quite unable to speak, although he would make certain sounds intended to convey his thoughts. It was soon found that his moral passions had undergone a change, and that from a particularly quiet, modest, and well-behaved inoffensive man, he had become indecent, exposing his person, revengeful, and spiteful. His mind soon gave way, he became imbecile and quite unmanageable, and it was soon found necessary to remove him to the Borough Asylum.

1868, *July 9th.*—I visited him to-day at the Asylum, and found him seated on a bench. He evidently recognised me, but was quite unable to speak a single word, and he evinced the greatest distress at his inability to converse with me. He had gained flesh, and looked well. Mr. Sutton, the resident medical officer, reported to me that about four months ago he had a series of epileptiform convulsions lasting forty-eight hours, and that he was, to all appearance, dying; he, however, soon recovered from this condition, but continued very helpless and unable to walk or even stand without assistance, although when supported by two persons he could walk a considerable distance. Mr. Sutton further reported that although unable to articulate, he gesticulates frightfully, and thus endeavours by the language of signs to supply the loss of articulate language. In further illustration of his psychological condition, I would add that his sister informs me that some months since, upon the occasion of his nephew playing the cornet in his presence, he, supported by two women, danced to the tune.*

---

* Since the above was written, this patient has died; the *post-mortem* appearances are given in detail in Part VI.

The above case seems to me to be pregnant with
material for careful thought and study, and if I have
dwelt thus minutely on its daily progress, it is because
I apprehend that it is not common to have the opportunity of watching for so long a time a patient presenting such an exceptional chain of symptoms. I shall
now proceed to analyse the various phases which the
clinical history of this man has from time to time
presented.

The sequence of morbid action here is curious. The
very first morbid symptom was total loss of speech;
after partial recovery of the faculty of speech, verbal
amnesia was observed—loss of the memory of words
limited to substantives—then epileptiform convulsions,
and, alternating with each other, hemiplegia and paraplegia; and eventually this curious chain of symptoms
merged into a state of general paralysis.

The loss of speech was, in the first instance, of the
ataxic form, for no amount of prompting would help
him. As the abolition of speech was complete, it is,
however, impossible to say whether or not there was at
this time verbal amnesia also. Probably there was, for
when the ataxic symptoms gave way, loss of the
memory of words was soon observed. Dr. William
Ogle* mentions two cases in which, after recovery from
the ataxic form of aphasia, amnemonia remained, which
he thinks must have co-existed at the earlier stage with
the ataxia; in both Dr. Ogle's cases, however, there was

---

* On Aphasia and Agraphia, St. George's Hosp. Reports, Vol. ii.,
1867. This interesting and highly instructive communication contains
the careful analysis of twenty-five cases, which have furnished
Dr. Ogle with the material for one of the most useful papers that
have been published on this subject.

hemiplegia, indicating a much more extensive lesion of brain than could have been suspected at this stage of Sainty's history.

The next feature to which I wish to call attention is, that not only was the total loss of speech the earliest symptom, but it was for some days the sole symptom. There was no paralysis—there was simply privation of the power of speech; it was simple aphasia, in the rigorous sense of the term—and cases such as this would seem to show that the faculty of speech may perish, or be suspended, *alone*, and that this faculty is special and independent.

The muscular apparatus, the instrument which served for the articulation of words, was in a perfect state of integrity; but an indispensable element was wanting. When the aphasia had assumed the amnesic form, the defect was dependent on loss of the memory of words; but in the earlier stage, when the ataxic form was present, was the defect due to the loss of the memory of the movements necessary for speech?

The complete but temporary loss of speech in the early stage, I presume was the result of a simple ephemeral cerebral congestion, probably situated in the same part of the brain as that, which being subsequently more seriously injured, gave rise to the more permanent symptoms.

I think we may assume that the disease was limited to the convolutional grey matter, as there never was any persistent paralytic symptom indicative of lesion of the central ganglia. The occurrence of paraplegic symptoms after one fit, and of hemiplegic symptoms after another, is worthy of notice. I will not attempt to offer any theoretical speculation as to the cause of

the temporary loss of motor power in the lower limbs;
I simply notice it as singular and exceptional. The
transitory hemiplegia, I presume, can be explained on
the supposition of temporary obstruction, or rather
spasm, of the middle cerebral artery, and the term
hemispasm, as suggested by Dr. Hughlings Jackson,
would be more appropriate to such a condition than
hemiplegia.

I wish to call particular attention to the fact that the
lesion which could produce total abolition of speech for
a considerable time, did not in the least impair the
intellect, for when he came under my care some months
afterwards, he seemed possessed of more intelligence
than most men of his class. I may here remark that
the opinion of those who have written upon this subject
is divided, as to whether the intelligence is, as a rule,
affected in aphasia. Trosseau held the opinion that the
mental faculties were always more or less impaired; on
the other hand, the case of Professor Lordat has been
cited as a proof that the aphasic condition may exist
with the highest amount of intellectual activity. It
seems that the illustrious Montpellier professor was at a
certain period of his life affected with aphasia, and he
has himself stated that, although speechless, he experienced no restraint or difficulty in the exercise of
thought and imagination. He prepared his lessons, he
arranged his subject, and was able mentally to dwell on
the salient points. "*Je possédais complétement, dit-il, la
partie interne du langage, je n'en avais perdu que la partie
externe.*"

The question has arisen in my own mind, as to
whether, during the early part of Sainty's illness, he
was capable of making a will? The solution of this

medico-legal question of the testamentary capacity of aphasics I will leave to the alienist physician.*

AMNESIC APHASIA, WITH RIGHT HEMIPLEGIA ; SOFTENING OF POSTERIOR PART OF LEFT HEMISPHERE ; ANTERIOR LOBES HEALTHY.

On the 20th of March, 1867, I was requested to see Mr. N——, a merchant, æt. 51, who, for a period of three or four months, had experienced abnormal symptoms, indicating want of brain power. For some time previous to this date, his friends noticed that he had become unusually quiet, less communicative, and dull. Shortly before Christmas, he had a sort of fainting fit, and soon afterwards he began to get confused in his conversation ; he would let objects drop from his right hand, and do awkward things at the table—on one occasion he poured vinegar on his repast instead of pepper. It was soon observed that he could not write a letter. From inquiries which I instituted in reference to his habits, it seems that he had led a fairly temperate and steady life, and that the only cause which could be assigned was the excitement and mental tension resulting from an entire change of occupation ; he having a few years previously exchanged the comparatively mechanical and automatic life of a country village, for a business of a speculating character in a large town, necessitating railway journeys to London twice a week.

During my somewhat lengthened interview with him, he never initiated any subject of conversation. When I questioned him, he seemed to get confused, and was conscious of this confusion, saying he could not find words to describe his symptoms. What answers he made, however, were given quite coherently, but in the fewest possible words. He seemed to understand

* M. Legrand du Saulle, in a course of lectures delivered at l'Ecole Pratique at Paris, during the summer of 1868, entered very fully into this subject, quoting instances of the serious difficulties which may arise from the testamentary acts of aphasics, who, although retaining full possession of their intelligence, may be totally incapacitated for making a will. (De l'état mentale necessaire pour faire une donation ou un testament—Gazette des Hôpitaux, June and July, 1868).

everything that was said, but he had, to a certain extent, lost the memory of words, and would call things by their wrong names—for instance, being in a room where the fire was burning particularly brightly, he said, "How bright the poker looks." The person to whom he was speaking said, "You mean the fire." "Yes," he said, "I mean the fire." He would be thus confused in the choice of words to express his thoughts, and the knowledge of this defect was a source of distress to him. The idea was conceived, but the means of communication with the external world did not exist. He complained of numbness in the right arm and leg, and the tactile power of the right hand was impaired. The heart's impulse was feeble, with no abnormal sound; the pupils were sluggish, and he complained of frequent dizziness and of frontal headache. His pale and pasty aspect, diminished secretion of urine, and other symptoms, caused me to deem it necessary to look carefully into the condition of the kidneys. The analysis of the urine gave the following results:—quantity passed in 24 hours, 26 ounces; sp. gr. 1·030, no albumen, some pale lithates. A microscopic examination revealed the presence of amorphous lithates, a few oxalates, and several oil globules and fat cells.

Chlorides - - -	4	parts per 1000
Urea - - -	16	,, ,,
Phosphoric acid, in combination	3·2	,, ,,

The condition of this patient was not materially altered for some weeks, when, after dressing himself one morning, he was profusely sick, and his symptoms suddenly culminated into an apoplectiform seizure, with right hemiplegia and total loss of speech, the latter symptom being the result of a state of coma, from which he never rallied.

Autopsy.—There was considerable congestion of the veins on the convex surface of the brain, but there was no opacity of membranes or other morbid appearance, either on the upper surface or at the base. The vessels composing the circle of Willis, and the arteries generally, were quite healthy, both cerebral arteries being specially examined and traced along the fissure of Sylvius, without any abnormal appearance being detected. At the point of union of the middle third with the posterior third of the convex surface of the left hemisphere, was a dilatation, or bulging out of the arachnoid, giving the appearance of a cyst. This contained at least two drachms of serum, the evacuation of which disclosed a tolerably well circumscribed portion of softened cerebral tissue, of about the size and shape of an apricot, with its upper segment depressed, so as to form a cup-shaped cavity. It was here the serum was lodged, and there was at this spot an actual destruction of cerebral matter; the softened tissue was of a yellowish grey colour, resembling a strong solution of gelatine in appearance. In the centre of this softened portion was a very small clot, or rather layer, of black blood, of about the size of an ordinary wafer. From the small size of the clot, and the great extent of the softening, it must be inferred that the softening preceded, and was the cause of the clot, and the recent date of the sanguineous effusion would also favour this view. The frontal convolutions were examined with great care, especially the third, and the substance between it and the corpus striatum, but these structures were found quite healthy. The disease was, in fact, limited to the posterior third of the left hemisphere.

The heart was covered with an unusual layer of external fat; its muscular substance was pale and flabby, and its walls attenuated. The kidneys were healthy, but congested, and somewhat below the normal size. The spleen was very soft and friable.

Doubtless it will be said by some that this is scarcely a case of aphasia. It is certainly by no means a typical instance of the affection, like the preceding case; but as I am treating of lesion as well as loss of speech, I think it deserves recording as an instance of the loss of the memory of words and impairment of the faculty of language, dependant upon softening of the posterior part of the left hemisphere, with perfect integrity of the frontal convolutions and of the anterior lobe generally. In the former part of this essay, I have already cited a case of Abercrombie, somewhat resembling this, and where the softening was also found in the *posterior* part of the left hemisphere.

RIGHT AND SUBSEQUENTLY LEFT HEMIPLEGIA, WITH LESION OF SPEECH. FRONTAL CONVOLUTIONS SOUND.

John Sutherland, a shoemaker, aged 60, was admitted into the Norfolk and Norwich Hospital, *December* 22nd, 1866, with the following history. He had not been a drinking man, had smoked very little, had suffered from gonorrhœa, but had never had syphilis or rheumatic fever. Whilst at work on *September 4th*, he suddenly lost the entire use of his right side, and also of his speech. The loss of articulate language was almost complete for about a fortnight, at the expiration of which time he could just make himself understood by those who knew him well; the partial recovery of his speech coincided with a little returning motor power in the leg, but it was not till two months later that there was any improvement in the hand.

Condition on admission.—There is still considerable loss of power in the right arm, and the forearm is contracted on the arm; he walks with difficulty, but there is less impairment in the use of the leg than the arm.

The memory and intellect are unaffected; he answers questions remarkably readily, and there is now no hesitation in his speech, but he speaks in a muffled, unnatural tone, as if the mouth was full. There is no evidence of cardiac disease, no unilateral sweating; he fancies he cannot smell as well as before the attack.

There was nothing in the treatment of this case to record, except that some weeks after his admission, galvanism was twice applied to the right leg, but this seemed to aggravate his condition, for in a few days there was complete paralysis of this limb.

Some days later he had a severe apoplectic seizure, resulting in paralysis of the entire *left* side, with great difficulty of speech, and he died in a few days.

A most careful *post mortem* examination was made, which I will not describe in detail; suffice it to say that the loss of motor power on the two sides was explained by a clot in the central part of each hemisphere; there was no obstruction of the middle cerebral arteries, and we clearly satisfied ourselves that the frontal convolutions were in no wise affected.

Independently of the integrity of the frontal convolutions, there are one or two other points in this case calling for a passing remark. It will be observed that galvanism caused a decided aggravation in his symptoms. This powerful remedial agent cannot be used with too great caution and discrimination in cases of paralysis, and I take blame to myself for having allowed its use here; for the contracted state of the forearm was indicative of a state of irritation and of exalted polarity of the nervous tissues, likely to be aggravated by electrical stimulus. Although the increase of the dextral paralysis was unaccompanied by any fresh aphasic symptoms, it will be observed that the occurrence of left hemiplegia coincided with great difficulty of speech. Those who view cases partially, and distort them to suit their own notions, would, in a statistical table, put this down as a case of left hemiplegia with aphasia; whereas it is evident that the difficulty in speaking which occurred during the last few days of his life, was due to a semi-comatose condition, induced by sudden cerebral hæmorrhage, and which rapidly ended in death. I have recorded his fancied loss of smell, because I think it important in all cases to notice the state of the olfactory function.

APHASIA, WITH RIGHT HEMIPLEGIA; NO LESION OF ANTERIOR LOBES.

The subject of this case, Mr. C. G——, was a gentleman, aged 36, who had led a very gay life, and who had on several occasions been affected with a severe form of venereal disease; he had also suffered from rheumatic fever. For many years he had been at times the subject of great mental excitement, and even to some extent of mental delusions. There was no hereditary predisposition to insanity in his family, but two of his brothers were affected with paralysis of the right side, the paralysis being in one of them attended with considerable impairment of the speech. In the year 1865 he entered into the married state, and, four months afterwards, his habitually excited condition much increased, and it became necessary to place him in an asylum. He now soon began to hesitate in his speech, and to give evidence of the loss of the memory of words; his power of writing also became impaired. Some months later, he was suddenly attacked with convulsions, followed by right hemiplegia, with total loss of speech, and he died in a few days. I was invited by his medical attendant to be present at the autopsy, when there was found evidence of chronic thickening of the arachnoid, with congestion of the pia mater of the left side especially; there was no clot, no degeneration of cerebral matter; the anterior convolutions were especially examined, and found quite healthy. The most remarkable appearance that this examination disclosed, was a deposit of rough bony matter, exostosis, at the centre of the fossa corresponding to the middle lobe of the brain on the left side, and to this rough surface the cerebral membranes were slightly adherent.

In the absence of any more decided cause, I presume the diseased condition of bone might account for the convulsions; but the case is curious from the fact of the hemiplegia being so decided without any disease of the central ganglia, or of the hemispheres. The *fons et origo mali* was undoubtedly the syphilitic taint. The occurrence of dextral paralysis, with dysphasia, in his brother, is just worthy of observation; in the account of Dr. Scoresby Jackson's remarkable case, it is stated that another member of the same family was affected with lesion of speech and paralysis of the right side.*

* Dr. Sumpter, of Cley, has recorded in the "Lancet," of October 3rd, 1868, a brief note of two cases of Aphasia then under his care, in which the patients stood in the relation to each other of mother and daughter.

In reference to the subject under discussion, I wish more particularly to call attention to the fact that this and the two preceding cases may be considered as directly opposed to Professor Broca's theory; in all three the frontal convolutions were examined with a scrupulous care, and were found quite healthy, and in the case of Mr. N——, which was a marked instance of the amnesic form of aphasia, the lesion was not near the anterior lobe at all, being situated at the posterior part of the upper surface of the hemisphere. With every desire to avoid the common error of drawing definite conclusions from a limited number of observations, I would add that three negative cases, supported by *post-mortem* verification, go far to outweigh three hundred cases, apparently admitting of a different interpretation, but where no autopsy was made.

It is somewhat singular that in each of the above three cases, there existed an abnormal condition of the left side of the base of the skull. In one case, as above stated (Mr. C. G.), there was actual *disease* of bone; in the case of Mr. N—— there was an unusual development of that part of the petrous portion of the left temporal, which corresponds to the perpendicular semicircular canal; and in Sutherland's case, there was a remarkable bony prominence in the left middle fossa, not existing on the other side. It will doubtless be said that unsymmetrical development of the two sides of the skull is not uncommon. I quite admit this, and I desire simply to record what I have observed, without attempting to draw any inference from such observation. I cannot but think, however, that it would be extremely desirable, in future autopsies of persons who during life exhibited symptoms of lesion of speech, that the condition of the bones of the skull should be minutely examined, and any unusual appearances accurately recorded.

LOSS OF SPEECH, WITH PARAPLEGIA: SPINAL SYMPTOMS.

George Green, a shoemaker, æt. 38, was admitted into the Norfolk and Norwich Hospital, on February 10th, 1866. Has had syphilis, but never suffered from any rheumatic affection. His first symptom was pain in the forehead and dimness of vision, for which he was treated as an out-patient at University College Hospital in the early part of 1864; up to this period he had been a most inveterate smoker, which habit he at once discontinued, at the request of Dr. Wilson Fox. During the summer of 1864, whilst at work, he suddenly lost the power of speech, there being at the same time an aggravation of the habitual frontal pain, but no symptom of paralysis, and he resumed his work next day. The total cessation of speech lasted about twenty minutes or half an hour, when the only symptom in connection with the power of speech was a slight hesitation and embarrassment, which lasted three or four days, and then as far as his speech was concerned, he was as well as ever. In about three weeks after the above symptoms, he was obliged to discontinue his work in consequence of being seized with a tingling feeling running from the extremities of the right fingers, along the arm to the top of the shoulder, and up to the right angle of the mouth; there was evidently partial paralysis, as he could not hold anything, and there seems to have been anæsthesia, as he speaks of numbness and loss of feeling; the paralytic symptoms were entirely confined to the right upper extremity. These symptoms disappeared in about two hours, and he resumed his work, no treatment having been adopted. About January, 1865, he began to feel a tired sensation in his legs, as if he had been walking a long distance; at the same time he noticed some difficulty in passing his water, and an habitual constipation began to increase. Six months later, he again lost his speech whilst reading, the loss of the power of utterance being preceded by a swimminess in the

head and dimness of vision : he went to bed, fell asleep, and
after three hours woke with the speech restored, but only a
little embarrassed ; the next day all was right. He has never
had dysphagia, and when the power of speaking has been
suspended, the movements of the tongue have been unimpaired.

Symptoms on admission.—He is quite unable to stand or
walk without assistance ; there is no deviation of, or pain on
pressure over the spine, except slightly at the neighbourhood
of the lower dorsal vertebræ ; there is no paralysis of the upper
extremities, and the organs of special sense are unimpaired.
The tongue is furred, the bowels are constipated, rarely acting
more than once a week ; there is difficulty in passing his water,
but only at night when in the recumbent posture. There is no
evidence of cardiac disease.

In the absence of any positive therapeutic indication, and
with the possibility of his symptoms being due to a remote
syphilitic cause, I prescribed small doses of perchloride of
mercury, and a cathartic electuary at bedtime.

March 26th—For several days has not felt so well, has had
but very little sleep ; had an attack yesterday similar to his
former ones, but much slighter in degree—the speech was
affected for about two hours, but much less so than on former
occasions. He attributes his relapse to want of sleep ; he
complains to-day of tingling and numbness in the left little
finger, which has been present for four or five days.

He derived some slight benefit from treatment, and left the
hospital on the 12th of May. Thinking this a case in which
it was very desirable to ascertain in what proportions the
principal solid ingredients of the urine were present, I made a
careful volumetric analysis of that secretion a few days before
his discharge, with the following result :—

Chlorides	7·5 parts per 1000.
Urea	17 „ „
Phosphoric acid (in combination)	1·1 „ „

Quantity passed in 24 hours, four pints; sp. gr. 1014;
reaction, alkaline.

Re-admitted December 1st. Omitting unimportant details, I
pass on to January 19th, 1867, when I find the following
entry :—He awoke in the middle of last night, and found that

G

he had lost his speech, this phenomenon being preceded by violent pains in both brows, just above the external angular process. He feels the pain in his forehead to-day, but the speech is now all right.

22*nd.*—He has vomited some bilious matter, and had early this morning a tingling up the right arm up to the side of the mouth.

February 16*th.*—No marked difference in his symptoms since admission, except that there is now rather sharp pain caused by pressure over the 8th and 9th dorsal vertebræ, and from this spot downwards; for some weeks past also there has been pain at this region when not touched. This patient soon afterwards left the hospital, and I heard nothing more of him, till his father came one day to say he had died quite suddenly. I regret I was not permitted to make a *post-mortem* examination.

The history of this patient is suggestive of the caution with which we should accept any statistics based upon cases only casually observed, or which have been under observation but a short time. Had this case been reported in its early stage, when there were abnormal symptoms present in the right upper extremity, it would perhaps have been recorded by some enthusiastic aphasiographer, as a case of aphasia with imperfect right hemiplegia, and it would thus have been cited with others to prove the correctness of Dax's theory; whereas, as time elapsed and other links were added to the morbid chain, paraplegia set in, and in fact there never was really any persistent paralysis of the upper extremities.

I do not wish to indulge in any hypothetical speculations as to the seat of this man's disorder. There was never any persistent symptom pointing directly to cerebral disease; whereas the persistent paraplegia and loss of function of the bladder and rectum, together latterly with tenderness and pain at the lower part of the spine, justified me in looking upon his symptoms as due to disease of an insidious nature in the spinal cord.

I have already mentioned, in a former part of this essay, a case reported by Dr. Maty, in which impairment of speech was one of the symptoms of spinal disease, and Abercrombie* has related three cases in which lesion of speech was accompanied by spinal symptoms; in the first of these, there was found after death suppuration between the cord and its membranes, the brain being perfectly healthy; in the second case, no disease whatever was found either in the brain or spinal cord, or in the bones of the spine, although the symptoms during life were those ordinarily indicative of spinal disease; in the third case there was undefined suppuration of the cord.

Ataxic Aphasia occurring as a Climacteric Symptom.

Anna Maria Moore, æt. 47, a labourer's wife, of a strongly marked nervous temperament, came under my observation as an out-patient of the hospital on Nov. 9th, 1867. She was the mother of ten children, had miscarried two years previously, had never enjoyed her usual health since, and menstruation from that time had always been irregular and too frequent. In February she had a severe sore throat, with ulceration of the tongue and of the mucous membrane of the cheek; and during this attack she lost the power of speaking for three days. Her speech continued all right till June, when the throat became similarly affected as in February, but to a less extent, and she again lost her speech. This time, however, the defect was not of a transitory character, as on the former occasion, for

* On Disease of the Brain and Spinal Cord, pp. 333, 356, 410.

it continued up to the time of the admission into the out-patient department of the hospital.

On my asking her what ailed her, she could not make her-self understood; she seemed, however, to understand perfectly what I said to her; and there was an attempt to talk, resulting in a nervous, unintelligible stutter. She seemed to have the proper use of her tongue, which was protruded straight; deglutition and phonation were unimpaired. At the expiration of a week, finding there was no return of the power of speech, she became an in-patient of the hospital.

Nov. 11th (two days after admission).—At my visit to-day, to my astonishment, she addressed me quite naturally. On making inquiries, I ascertained that when first admitted into the ward nobody could understand her. On getting up the next day she found she could speak better; the improvement continued during the day, and this morning she speaks as well as ever.

Nov. 23rd—No return of her inability to speak having occurred, she was this day made out-patient.

1868. *Jan. 1st.*—Presented herself at the hospital to-day. The speech is impaired; she is, however, menstruating, and she says her speech is always more embarrassed at the period of menstruation.

Jan. 29th.—Speech very bad to-day; can only express herself with the greatest difficulty. Menstruation, which should have begun some days since, has not yet occurred.

Feb. 12th.—Menstruation still deferred. For a period of three days, since her last visit, she could scarcely speak at all.

Without dwelling on the further details of this case, I would merely observe that the urinary secretion varied considerably in quantity, and she seldom passed a fortnight without what she called "a stoppage"—evidently an attack of painful micturi-tion, with partial suppression. It seemed desirable to make a volumetric analysis of the urine, which gave the following result as to the principal solid ingredients:—

Chlorides	-	-	-	7 parts per 1,000
Urea	-	-	-	19 ,,
Phosphoric acid in combination	-		1.8 ,,

Quantity passed in 24 hours 3½ pints, sp. gr. 1020, freely acid, no albumen. In reference to the treatment of this case, I found diffusive stimulants of service, and she subsequently derived considerable benefit from the bromide of potassium.

On analysing this patient's symptoms, it is clear that the defect of the speech was ataxic—for no amount of prompting could assist her in the least; there was no amnesia. What was wanted was not the word, but the recollection of the process by which to give it utterance. I do not apprehend that the faculty of language was impaired in its intimate seat, for she was in no wise deprived of ideas necessary to serve as a pabulum for language, but there was suspension of the power of co-ordination necessary to the production of speech. I presume the embarrassment of speech was due to what M. Auguste Voisin* calls, " *l'interruption plus ou moins complète de l'incitation volontaire*," or, to use the words of Todd, " There did not exist that relation between the centre of volition and that of intellectual action which is necessary to give expression to the thoughts in suitable language; the centre of intellectual action had full power to frame the thoughts, but as the will was not prompted to a certain mode of sustained action, the organs of speech could not be properly brought into play."

The fact of the dysphasia being aggravated at the menstrual periods is worthy of notice. It first occurred after a menorrhagic flux, and the whole morbid chain of symptoms may be considered as climacteric. M.

* This accomplished alienist physician, to whom I am much indebted for great personal courtesy during a recent visit to La Salpêtrière, is the author of an excellent article on Aphasia in "Le Nouveau Dictionnaire de Médecine et de Chirurgie Pratique."

Delasiauve has cited the case of a lady who for three years, at each menstrual period, was affected with mutism and partial paraplegia, being at those times only able to make herself understood by signs.*

Another interesting feature in this case to which I would call attention, without, however, drawing any inference from it, is—that the lesion of speech first occurred after a severe attack of sore throat. I regret I have not been able to ascertain whether the throat affection was of a diphtheritic character, but the coincidence of the two symptoms is deserving of notice.

It may, perhaps, be said that cases like the above are common enough; possibly they are, but their study is not the less interesting on that account; and here I would ask what was the ultimate cause of the symptoms observed in this patient? I have heard the term nervousness applied to such cases, but this word throws no light on their pathology. Nervousness, like hysteria, is a word frequently used as a cloak to our ignorance.

Is it not possible that the abnormal symptoms might be due to some form of uræmic poisoning? There were two circumstances rather favouring this view— viz., the partial retention of a fluid which had for years been periodically thrown off, and the frequent partial suppression of the urinary secretion. In reference to this latter hypothesis, it is true that the volumetric analysis of the urine (made at a time when the secretion was in its normal quantity) did not disclose a predominance of any particular ingredient; still, I cannot help thinking that in this and similar cases, where the symptoms are intermittent, they may be due to

---

* Journal de Médecine Mentale, 1865.

some element in the blood which has a deleterious effect upon the cerebral circulation.

It will be observed that there is no abolition of a faculty in such cases as the above, but simply an obstacle to the manifestation of such faculty. The faculty of language is present, but one of the processes is wanting by which it is brought into communication with the external world.

LEFT HEMIPLEGIA WITH APHASIA; NO DISEASE OF FRONTAL CONVOLUTIONS; EXTENSIVE DISEASE OF RIGHT HEMISPHERE; VEGETATIONS ON AORTIC AND MITRAL VALVES; FIBRINOUS BLOCKS IN THE SPLEEN.

William Lemon, a gasfitter, æt. 40, was admitted into the Norfolk and Norwich Hospital on January 4, 1868, with the following antecedent history;—He had been ailing more or less since Midsummer, but had been able to continue his work till early in November. A fortnight later, he was suddenly seized with left hemiplegia, and considerable embarrassment of speech, to such an extent that a stranger could not understand him at all. His power of speech gradually improved, and at the end of a fortnight he could speak nearly as well as usual.

Condition on admission.—There is complete motor paralysis of left leg and arm; anæsthesia only partial, if any. He has no pain or abnormal sensation in the head, and the organs of special sense are unimpaired, and there now remains but very slight embarrassment in his speech. Urine sp. gr. 1023, freely acid, slightly albuminous, and loaded with lithates. There is a well-marked double bruit heard nearly all over the anterior part of the chest, but at its maximum intensity at the apex, the diastolic murmur being the most marked. Pulse 84, quite steady and regular, but very hard, sharp, and almost dicrotic.

January 18*th.*—This patient continued much the same as on admission up to 6 p.m. yesterday, when the nurse, on taking him his tea, noticed he had lost the power of articulation,

although he seemed to know all that was going on; a few
minutes before the power of speech was lost he spoke a few
words, implying that he saw imaginary beings around his bed.
The power of articulation was never recovered, and he soon
became comatose, and died early this morning.

Autopsy.—Heart: weight 19 oz.; right ventricle contained
coloured and decolorised clots extending just beyond the pulmonary valves; right auriculo-ventricular orifice admitted four
fingers and a thumb; tricuspid valves healthy; walls of left
ventricle immensely hypertrophied; dilatation of left auriculo-
ventricular orifice; the mitral and aortic valves were both
covered with fibrinous vegetations, apparently recent; there
was commencing atheroma to the extent of an inch and three
quarters at the origin of the aorta.   Liver: weight 4lbs. 2 oz.,
healthy.   Kidneys; the right weighed 11½ oz., the left 8 oz.,
both in a state of intense congestion.   Spleen: very soft and
friable, contained several fibrinous blocks.   Brain: stripped of
dura mater, it weighed 3lbs. 8½ oz.; there was no abnormal
vascularity or other morbid appearance, either on its convex
surface or at the base.   There was a general flattening of the
superior surface of the right hemisphere, which was somewhat
less developed than the left, and its convolutions were shrunk.
The brain was carefully sliced, and no abnormal appearance
disclosed until opening the lateral ventricles, when a yellow
stain was seen on the upper portion of the right corpus
striatum; on a level with this body, but behind, and external
to it—at about the middle third of the hemisphere—was a
softened portion of about the size and shape of a large walnut;
there was also slight softening of the thalamus at its posterior
part.   On cutting into the corpus striatum it was seen that the
posterior two-thirds had undergone the softening process, being
of a yellowish hue, and waxy consistency.   Antero-posterior
slices were made in both anterior lobes, but no morbid change
revealed; the frontal convolutions were examined with great
care, and the right and left convolutions compared, but they
seemed perfectly healthy; but as the softening of the right
hemisphere approached so near the surface of the right side—
certainly within half an inch of the third frontal convolution—
it is quite possible that some slight alteration of the posterior
part of the frontal convolutions may have existed, not patent to
our means of investigation.   The vertebral and basilar arteries
were healthy, as also the termination of the carotids.   There

was no obstruction of the middle cerebral arteries, but that on the right side, when traced along the fissure of Sylvius, presented at the point of its first bifurcation a milky appearance, to the extent of about a quarter of an inch in length. The olivary bodies were specially examined, and were quite healthy, as were also the medulla oblongata, cerebellum, pons, and crura cerebri.

Microscopic Examination.—A separate examination was made of the corpus striatum, and also of the softened hemisphere. In the corpus striatum there was no proper brain structure ; an absence of vessels and nerve fibres ; an abundance of granular matter. In the portion taken from the hemisphere there was an absence of nerve fibres, and the vessels were coloured with fawnish pigment ; there was an abundance of granular matter, with here and there a fat globule.

The above case is extremely interesting from several points of view. In the first place, I would observe that the cardiac disease was doubtless the primary cause of the softening of the cerebral tissue ; and it is extremely probable that some vegetations, similar to those observed on the aortic and mitral valves, had become detached, and thus had been carried into one or more of the cerebral vessels, although no positive evidence of obstruction existed after death.

The condition of the spleen is confirmatory of this view, as the fibrinous blocks found in that organ undoubtedly betokened an obstruction to the splenic circulation similar to that which had probably produced the cerebral symptoms. It would seem that these fibrinous deposits in the spleen have been frequently observed in the autopsies of aphasic patients. In four of Dr. Wm. Ogle's cases this condition of spleen was observed ; and in each case—as in that of Lemon—there was also disease of the heart.

It will be observed that the lesion of speech was

associated with paralysis of the *left* side. This coincidence of aphasia with left hemiplegia is, I believe, much more common than is generally supposed. I have at the present time an instance of it under my care at the Norwich Hospital, and I have already, in the preceding pages, mentioned cases where this combination of symptoms was observed. Dr. Crichton Browne has informed me that he has collected six cases of left hemiplegia with aphasia, which I trust he may be induced to place on record.

If the above observation is in direct antagonism to M. Dax's theory of the localisation of speech in the left hemisphere, it is *a fortiori* opposed to that of Professor Broca; for although the softening was suspiciously near the third frontal convolution of the *right* side, the *left* frontal convolutions, as indeed the entire left hemisphere, presented no trace of disease whatever.

I could mention several other most interesting cases which have lately fallen under my own observation, where loss or lesion of the faculty of articulate language was a prominent symptom, but this part of my essay has already far exceeded its original limits, and I trust that the observations I have recorded may have been sufficiently varied to illustrate the clinical history of aphasia. I shall, therefore, now proceed to the consideration of certain abstract points suggested by an analytical study of the cases mentioned in the preceding pages, and for the accomplishment of this task I shall have to avail myself of the assistance of the sister sciences—Physiology and Comparative Anatomy.

PART IV.

In the preceding pages I have endeavoured to review what is at present known of the clinical history of aphasia; having first ventured critically to analyse a certain number of cases recorded by independent observers in various parts of the world, I have then minutely detailed several cases which I have myself had the opportunity of personally watching.

It will be observed that the observations which I have recorded in illustration of my subject have been of the most varied character—from the typical case where the loss of speech was complete, to that where the loquelar defect was only a slight or even an occasional symptom, believing that it is only by the careful study of cases illustrative of the various forms and degrees in which derangement of the faculty of speech is observed, that we can hope to throw any light upon this much disputed question—the localisation of the Faculty of Speech.

I shall now proceed to dwell upon certain abstract points suggested by the consideration of the 72 cases to which I have referred in the former parts of this essay.. In the first place, it may be said that it is

unwise to study aphasia as if it were a malady *per se* ;
it is clearly only a symptom, and not a pathological
entity having a proper place in any nosological classification.   Whilst fully admitting this, however, I main-
tain that, for the purposes of scientific inquiry, it is
convenient at present to study loss of speech—as many
other investigators are doing—as if it were really a
morbid entity; for in many of the cases I have reported
it was the sole abnormal symptom present.   Besides,
the faculty of articulate language is the great distinction
which the Creator has made between man and the lower
animals; it is one of the highest of human attributes,
and there is no subject more worthy of the attention of
the philosophical physician than the investigation into
the causes which interfere with the proper use of this
faculty.   I shall, therefore—as it were under protest,
and as a matter of convenience—consider aphasia
under the various heads of Causes, Varieties, Treatment, &c.

SYNONYMS.—Few subjects in medical philology have
given rise to so much discussion as the name by which
loss of the faculty of articulate language should be
scientifically designated; a brief allusion, therefore, to
the various names proposed cannot be omitted.   The
term Anaudia was used by the Greek physicians for
loss of speech, and the adjective ἄναυδος is employed by
Æschylus.*   Alalia is used by Sauvages, Frank, and

* " αἰθερία κόνις με πείθει φανεῖσ',
     ἄναυδος, σαφής, ἔτυμος ἄγγελος."
                    SEPTEM CONTRA THEB, V. 81.
  "You' cloud of dust that choaks the air,
   A true tho' tongueless messenger."

others, and Professor Lordat* in describing his own case employed the word "*Alalie*," which latter term has also been adopted by M. Jaccoud. In 1861, M. Broca, when relating to the Anatomical Society of Paris his two remarkable cases, which have since excited so much interest throughout the scientific world, used the word "*Aphémie*" (a φημι). This last expression has latterly given way to *Aphasia*, a word adopted by M. Trousseau, who is supported in his preference for it by no less an authority than M. Littre.† Other names such as Aphrasia, Aphthongia, Aphthenxia, &c., have been suggested.‡ Aphasia, doubtless from its simplicity and euphony, is now the favourite expression; it is the one I have selected, and in accordance with the neological phraseology of the day, I shall adopt the terms—Amnesic, Ataxic, and Epileptiform Aphasia, &c.

DEFINITION.—The word aphasia has been used in a different sense by different authors; some, like Trousseau, Broca, Auguste Voisin, &c., limit its use to

* "Analyse de la Parole pour servir à la théorie de divers cas d'Alalie et de Paralalie." 1843.

† This word occurs twice in Homer; Iliad xvii., 695; and Odyss. iv., 704; the text being precisely the same in both instances— "δὴν δε' μιν ἀμφασίη ἐπέων λάβε;" here speechlessness from emotional causes is evidently implied.

‡ Dr. Popham, of Cork, considers that of all the words in the Greek language denoting modes of speech, the verb φθέγγομαι applies more than any of the others to the formation by the tongue of articulate sounds. The substantive φθέγξις is used by Hippocrates, and the privative word αφθέγξίς would express an inability to enunciate syllables. He also thinks that the English word aphthenxia is as euphonious as many other derivations from the Greek.—*Dublin Quarterly Journal,* November, 1865.

designate that condition in which the intelligence is
unaffected, or at all events but slightly impaired;
where thoughts are conceived by the patient, but he
cannot express himself, either because he has lost the
memory of words, or because he has lost the memory of
the mechanical process necessary for the pronunciation
of these words; or because the rupture of the means of
communication between the grey matter of the brain
and the organs whose co-operation is necessary to produce speech, does not allow the will to act upon them
in a normal manner—the ideas are formed, but the
means of communication with the external world do
not exist. This definition would exclude all cases in
which loss or lesion of speech was due to the alteration
of the peripheral organs which co-operate for the production of sounds, as well as those in which the embarrassment of speech was attributable to a general
lesion of the intelligence, such as idiotism, cretinism,
deaf-mutism and the different forms of mental aliena-
tion.

I prefer, however, using the word in its strictly
etymological sense—a φασισ—and I would thus apply
it to all cases where speech is abolished or suppressed
from whatsoever cause, believing that it is more convenient for the purposes of pathological research, thus
to consider lesion of speech in its general and widest
sense. This interpretation of the word necessitates
divisions and sub-divisions in which all shades and
degrees of the affection may be included, and it has
enabled me, in the preceding pages, not only to admit
cases where the lesion of speech was decided and more
or less permanent, but also those where it appeared
only as an epiphenomenon, believing, as I have before

stated, that such cases may be more useful than the typical cases which are so frequently put on record.

Before alluding to any subdivision of the subject, I would, just for one moment, ask what speech is ?

Speech is a complex faculty consisting of two distinct elements, one physical, somatic, and material—a movement; the other psychical, the interior speech—the λόγος; and we must take care not to confound this inward with the outward speech or articulation, which is only a form of expression. Here I must remark that it is important not to confound the *faculty of articulate language* with the *general faculty of language*, and Professor Broca's remarks on this subject are so lucid and terse, and of such a philosophical character, that I cannot do better than transcribe them.—" There are several kinds of language ; every system of signs which permits the expression of ideas in a manner more or less intelligible, more or less complete, or more or less rapid, is a language in the general sense of the word : thus speech, mimicry, dactylology, writing both hieroglyphic and phonetic, are so many kinds of language. There is a general faculty of language which presides over all these modes of expression of thought, and which may be defined—the faculty of establishing a constant relation between an idea and a sign, be this sign a sound, a gesture, a figure, or a drawing of any kind. Moreover, each kind of language necessitates the play of certain organs of emission and reception. The organs of reception are at one time the ear, at another the eye, and sometimes the touch. As to the organs of emission, they are brought into play by voluntary muscles such as those of the larynx, of the

tongue, of the velum palati, of the face, of the upper
limbs, &c. Every regular language, then, presupposes
the integrity : 1st—of a certain number of muscles, of
motor nerves which supply them, and of that part of
the nervous system from which these nerves arise ;
2nd—of a certain external sensorial apparatus, of the
sensitive nerve which supplies it, and of that part of
the central nervous system with which this nerve is
connected ; 3rd—of that part of the brain which presides
over the general faculty of language, such as it has just
been defined. The absence or abolition of this faculty
renders all kinds of language impossible."*

The elementary form of language which exists from
earliest infancy, and amongst all people and races, is
gesture ; the child points to certain objects and persons,
this being a sign of recognition of something that had
previously made an impression on the optic nerve—in
fact a proof is given of the existence of the faculty of
memory ; the parent now steps in, and the child is
taught to connect certain objects and persons with certain conventional signs or symbols called words, and
in order to effect this the auditory apparatus must
concur, and speech is the result—the faculty of articulate language is for the first time roused into action.

Certain conditions, however, are indispensable for the
development of articulate language : 1st—there must
be integrity of thought, or at all events an idea must
be conceived ; or, as Mr. Dunn elegantly remarks,
"must be moulded for expression in the seat of intellectual actions." 2nd—there must be a connexion
between the idea conceived, and the conventional signs

"Sur le Siége de la Faculté du Langage Articulé," p. 4.

or symbols which constitute the verbal forms of language. 3rd—the idea being conceived and the verbal form found, there must be integrity of the commissural fibres and of the motor centres through which the volitional impulses operate in speech, and the muscles of phonation and of articulation must be able to obey the mandates of the will. 4th—it would seem that all these conditions may exist, and yet there may be aphasia or dysphasia. One of my own cases, that of Anna Maria Moore, is a good illustration of this fact; she had plenty of ideas, she knew the symbols which corresponded to them—the representative signs of her thoughts—and the muscles of phonation and of articulation were unaffected, but she seemed like an accomplished musician, who, although accustomed to perform rapid and difficult passages upon his instrument with the greatest ease and without any conscious effort, suddenly finds himself, under certain unfavourable conditions of excitement or from the abuse of alcoholic stimulants, only able to produce discordant strains—there lacks our fourth condition, the master mind, or what has lately been called *the power of co-ordination*.

The child is taught to speak, as he is taught to walk, and he only speaks because he has been taught; what he has learned to do he can forget, and aphasia may be the result of the loss of the memory of the movements necessary for the articulation of words; thus it would seem that one can become aphasic in two ways, either by losing the memory of the symbols of language, or by forgetting the mechanical movements necessary to give expression to such symbols.

H

CLASSIFICATION.—The various authors who have written on loss or lesion of speech have each adopted a different classification. I have already alluded to the three divisions of Dr. Jules Falret; M. Jaccoud makes five;* Dr. Popham, of Cork, says that two typical forms are to be discriminated—*Lethological or Amnesic Aphasia*, and *Aneural or Ataxic Aphasia;* adding, that to these two forms there are cognate states, between which and them it is not easy at times to draw the line of demarcation.† The idea of this division has been further amplified by Dr. William Ogle, in the admirable essay to which I have before alluded, in which he defines by the term *Amnemonic Aphasia* that form characterized by loss of the memory of words— by inability to translate ideas into symbols; but besides this, he says, a second act of memory is required, closely connected with the former, yet distinct from it. "Not only must we remember words, but we must also re- member *how to say them.* The mere memory of words by itself may produce an inward repetition or mental rehearsal of a phrase, but it can do no more; for the utterance of the phrase in articulate sound this second memory is absolutely requisite." To the failure of this second memory Dr. Ogle gives the name of *Atactic Aphasia*, adding that the loss of speech is due to the want of the co-ordinating power over the muscles of articulation.‡

At the annual meeting of the British Association, held in Norwich last summer, Professor Broca, in proposing the adoption of a more precise terminology

* "Gazette Hebdomadaire," 1864.
† "On Aphasia," p. 5.
‡ St. George's Hospital Reports, Vol. 2, 1867, p. 95.

for expressing the various forms of defective speech, suggested the following divisions:—*Alogia*, loss of speech from defective intelligence; *Amnesia*, from defective memory of words; *Aphemia*, from a defect in the special faculty of language; and *Alalia*, from defective articulation.*

Although I have found it useful to adopt the terms *Amnesic* and *Ataxic Aphasia* in the description of my own cases, I do not wish to fetter myself with any system of classification, which must, to a certain extent, be artificial; I propose, however, under the head of " *Varieties*," to mention the principal forms of the affection which are most commonly met with by the clinical observer.

VARIETIES.—There is a great diversity in the particular type or form in which lesion of speech may shew itself, for as it is a symptom and not a malady *per se*, we cannot expect to find the same uniformity in its manifestation as is to be met with in the description of a specific and well characterized disease; having no uniform cause, it has no regular stereotyped march, being only a secondary pathological phenomenon, the result of single or multiple organic lesions.

* One of the most interesting features of the Norwich meeting—at all events, to the medical profession—was the discussion which followed the reading of papers on Aphasia by Dr. Hughlings Jackson, Mr. Dunn, and M. Broca. The learned Parisian Professor, with great force and eloquence, expounded before a British audience, his own peculiar views as to the seat of speech, illustrating his remarks by a coloured diagram, and a plaster cast. A most animated debate ensued, in which Professor Hughes Bennett, Professor Humphry, Dr. Crisp, Sir Duncan Gibb, Professor Carl Vogt, and others took a part. It may be said of this discussion—*Tot homines tot sententiæ.*

1.—It may differ in degree, from absolute speechlessness to various grades of imperfection in the use of the faculty of language; it may be an ephemeral and intermittent symptom, or it may be a permanent defect.

2.—Some persons have only lost the power of saying their own name (Crichton), or the names of other people; it is not uncommon to find persons whose conversation is perfect with the single exception that they cannot evoke or call up in their mind certain individuals—they lack the symbol necessary to convey the idea; it may perhaps be said that this defect is only one of the signs of senile decay—of the failing memory of elderly people; this view, however, does not furnish any explanation of the fact of the defect being limited to proper names; besides, this form occurs in others than in elderly people.

3.—In another variety the defect applies to substantives generally, as was observed in the man Sainty whose case I have myself recorded; I have also given several other instances of it in the preceding pages (Bergmann, Graves, &c.); and in many of these cases, the defect is supplied by a paraphrase, as was observed in Dr. Bergmann's case, where the patient being unable to say scissors, said, *it is what we cut with.* It is indeed singular that substantives and proper names which are first acquired by memory in childhood should be sooner forgotten than verbs, adjectives, and other parts of speech which are of a much later acquisition. In noticing this peculiarity, Dr. Osborne offers as an explanation, that nouns are less frequently repeated than verbs or prepositions, which, being in use on every

topic which can form the subject of discourse, are retained, when the names of general topics as nouns, or
of individual topics as proper names, are forgotten.*
In further illustration of this variety I would refer to a
case reported by M. Piorry, in which an old priest,
after an attack of dextral paralysis, had entirely lost
the faculty of employing substantives ; the manner in
which he expressed himself was most curious—for
instance, if he wished to ask for his hat, this unfortunate
word hat failed him entirely, and he made use of verbs,
pronouns, and adjectives in order to render his idea.
"Donnez-moi . . . ce qui se met sur la . . . mais le mot
tête ne lui venait pas ; il cherchait vingt fois à exprimer
sa pensée, et la chose lui présentait une difficulté insur-
montable."†

Perhaps one of the most curious forms in which imperfection of speech shews itself, is where the defect is
limited to some particular language ; thus Dr. Beattie
(quoted by Dr. Scoresby Jackson) mentions the case of
a gentleman, who, after a blow on the head, lost his
knowledge of Greek, and did not appear to have lost
anything else. Dr. S. Jackson asks—where was that
gentleman's Greek deposited, that it could be blotted
out by a single stroke, whilst his native language and
all else remained?‡ Professor Béhier's case, which I
have quoted in our first part, is a further illustration of

* "On the Loss of the Faculty of Speech." Dublin Journal of
Medical Science, Nov., 1833. This, after Crichton's, is one of the
earliest memoirs on our subject which have come under my notice, and
contains several highly interesting and well recorded cases.

† Gazette des Hôpitaux, May 27, 1865. At the autopsy of this
patient, M. Piorry found in the anterior part of the left corpus striatum
three apoplectic cysts.

‡ "Edinburgh Medical Journal," February, 1867.

this variety, his patient having entirely lost the use of two out of three languages that she had acquired.

4.—In another class we find patients substituting one word for another; thus Crichton's patient would ask for his boots when he wanted bread; the gentleman whose case was observed by Sir Thomas Watson, would say "pamphlet" for camphor; and in one of my own cases—that of C M—the patient would say "poker" when he meant the fire. In this erratic speech the defect is sometimes limited to the substitution of one letter for another, as in a case quoted by Crichton, where, after recovery from a fever, one of the first things the patient (a German) desired to have was coffee (kaffee); but instead of pronouncing the letter f, he substituted in its place a z, and therefore asked for a cat (kazze), and in every word which had an f, he committed a similar mistake, substituting a z for it.* Dr. Popham, of Cork, cites a similar example.

5.—A certain number of aphasics use stereotyped phrases, always the same, in answer to every question—thus we have seen in one of Trousseau's cases, that the patient thus addressed, invariably replied "*n'y a pas de danger;*" in Hasbach's case the phrase "*gerechter Gott*" was the only one at the command of the patient; others can only pronounce certain monosyllables—in one of Professor Broca's cases the word "*Tan,*" and in one of M. Charcot's the word "*Ta,*" composed the entire vocabulary of the respective patients; and in one of Dr. S. Jackson's, of Pennsylvania, we have seen that the patient, who was totally deprived of articulate speech, could write only the unintelligible phrase,

* "An Inquiry into Mental Derangement," Vol. i., p 373.

" *Didoes doe the doe.*" In many of these cases the play of the physiognomy shews that the sense of a question is perfectly understood by the patients; they have not lost the general faculty of language, for they understand written and articulate language when spoken by others; they preserve even the sense and the value of words, both in the auditive and graphic form; what is wanting in them is not the concurrence of the nerves and muscles engaged in phonation and articulation— for they can pronounce certain syllables spontaneously, and can sometimes repeat what is said to them—there is, however, wanting a particular faculty which we may call the faculty of articulate language; or, according to some authors, the faculty of co-ordinating the movements necessary for the production of articulate language is deficient.

A modern French philosopher, Paul Janet, mentions the case of an old priest who was incapable of pronouncing distinctly two words having any sense— " c'était à peine un bégayement ;" if, however, an appeal was made to his verbal memory, he could recite the fable of La Fontaine, " *Le Coche et la Mouche*," or the celebrated exordium of Father Bridaine, and this he would do with the most perfect distinctness of articulation, although he was evidently incapable of understanding a single word of what he said. In this case, says Paul Janet, the mnemonic mechanism had remained sound at a particular point, which only required stimulation to make it act.*

* "Le Cervean et la Pensée par Paul Janet. Membre de l'Institut." p. 140. This highly philosophical treatise contains much original matter, and is well worthy of a careful perusal by all medical psychologists who are endeavouring to trace the connexion between thought and speech.

6.—In another variety there is a remarkable perversion of speech; patients can articulate, but there is no connexion between the articulated sounds and the ideas which they may wish to convey. In illustration of this form, Dr. Osborne has related the history of a gentleman, who, after recovery from an attack of apoplexy, had the mortification of finding himself deprived of speech, or rather he spoke, but what he uttered was quite unintelligible, and his extraordinary jargon led to his being treated as a foreigner in the hotel at Dublin, where he stopped. In order to ascertain and place on record the peculiar imperfection of language which he exhibited, Dr. Osborne selected the following sentence from the by-laws of the College of Physicians, viz.—"*It shall be in the power of the College to examine or not to examine any Licentiate, previous to his admission to a Fellowship, as they shall think fit.*" Having requested him to read this aloud, he read as follows:—"*An the be what in the temother of the trothotodoo to majorum or that emidrate ein einkrastrai mestreit to ketra totombreidei to ra fromtreido asthat kekritest.*" Dr. Osborne calls attention to the fact, that although the patient appeared generally to know when he spoke wrong, yet he was unable to speak right, notwithstanding, as is proved from the above specimen, he articulated very difficult and unusual syllables, and was completely free from any paralytic affection of the vocal organs.*

Trousseau has recorded the case of a lady, who, without having ever experienced any paralytic symptom, was affected with the following strange perversion of speech. On receiving a call from a visitor, she rose to

* Osborne, op. citato., p. 160.

receive him with a benevolent smile on her countenance, and pointing to a chair, said—"*Pig, Brute, Stupid Fool.*" "Mrs. B— begs you to be seated," said a relative who was present, and who thus became the interpreter of the wishes of the patient thus strangely expressed. Trousseau adds that the acts of this lady seemed logical and sensible, and, strange to say, she did not seem to be aware of the foul language she was using.*

Dr. W. T. Moore, of Dublin, has also recorded a similar case of a gentleman, aged fifty-six, who, after an attack of hemiplegia, completely lost the connexion between ideas and words. On one occasion Dr. Moore was much puzzled by the patient saying to him— "*Clean my boots.*" Finding that he was not understood, he became much excited, and cried out vehemently —"*Clean my boots by walking on them!*" At length it was ascertained that the cause of his disquietude was the shining of the candle on his face, and that the object of his unintelligible sentences was to have the curtain drawn; when this was done he appeared quite gratified. This patient slowly improved from this attack, but became a lunatic, in which state he survived for fifteen or sixteen years. In commenting on this singular case, Dr. Moore calls attention to the fact that, although there was no connexion whatever between the words used and the ideas intended to be conveyed, this patient formed complete sentences: the power of co-ordination and of articulation was perfect, and the intelligence was, to all appearance, unimpaired.

Whilst these pages are passing through the press, my attention has been called to an extremely interesting case just published by Dr. Russell of Birmingham.

* Clinique Médicale, tom. ij., p. 576.

The subject of it, a cabman, with a constitution shattered by syphilis, after several epileptic fits, became affected with aphasia, the defect being greater in reading, many words in a sentence being changed or quite unintelligible. He could write his name correctly, but in writing from dictation, the perversion of language was so great that "*there was hardly an English word in the sentence, and much of the writing, like the gibberish spoken, was unreadable.*" At the autopsy, the left middle cerebral artery was found filled at its origin with a colourless unadherent plug of fibrin, which did not extend into the carotid ; all its branches were empty.[*]

For the description of cases of perverted speech, such as those just mentioned, Dr. Moore suggests the term Heterophasia.[†]

7.—The loss of speech may be the sole morbid symptom, or it may be accompanied by some paralytic symptom. A recent writer on nervous diseases, Dr. Wilks, has stated that pure aphasia without paralysis is uncommon.[‡] My own observation and researches do

[*] "British Medical Journal," Feb. 12th, 1870.

[†] "Dublin Quarterly Journal of Medical Science," Vol XL., p. 254 ; also Vol. XLVI., p. 487.

[‡] "On Aphasia and the education of the Cerebro-Spinal Centres." Med. Times, January 18th, 1868—"When paralysis exists, we believe that some portion of the motor tract must be affected, and that this need not arise from a local lesion of the cortical substance ; consequently it might be thought possible for hemiplegia to occur without loss of speech and *vice versa*, but I cannot find this is the case." Further on, Dr. Wilks says, "believing as I do that aphasia is almost invariably found with hemiplegia." It is with great diffidence that I venture to criticise the opinion of so eminent an authority as Dr. Wilks ; but the above statement is so utterly at variance with my own experience, that I cannot allow it to pass unnoticed.

not lead me to endorse this opinion, and amongst the
72 cases I have recorded, it will be observed that in a
large number the impairment of speech was the only
sign of diseased action (vide Andral, Broca, and Dr. S.
Jackson, of America). One of the most remarkable
instances of this variety was that recorded by Trousseau
when speaking of the aphasia of his colleague, Professor
Rostan. This case is of such value from the fact that
the subject of it had devoted a long life to the investigation of cerebral disease, and consequently was so well
qualified to appreciate, and accurately to describe the
symptoms he experienced in his own person, that I
shall transcribe it here.

"Dr. R——, being confined to his house from the effects of
an accident, had been reading nearly all day, and had thus
fatigued his brain. He was engaged in reading one of
Lamartine's literary conversations, when, all on a sudden, he
perceived that he imperfectly understood what he was perusing.
He stopped a moment, then resumed his reading, but again
experienced the same phenomenon. In his alarm, he wished
to call for assistance, when, to his great astonishment, he found
himself unable to speak a word. He now fancied himself the
subject of apoplexy, and he immediately caused his arms and
legs to execute various complex movements, and found there
was no paralysis. Being alone, he rang the bell, and when
his servant came, he found he could not speak a word. He
moved his tongue in all directions, and was struck with the
strange contrast which existed between the facility of movement
of the vocal organs, and the impossibility of giving expression
to his thoughts by speech. He now made a sign that he
wished to write; but when pen and ink were brought—although
he had the perfect use of his hand—he found himself quite as
unable to give expression to his thoughts by writing as by
speaking. On the arrival of a physician, at the end of two or
three hours, Dr. R—— turned up his sleeve, pointed to the
bend of the elbow, and clearly indicated that he wished to be
bled. Venesection was hardly finished, when a few words

could be uttered; by degrees the veil seemed to be removed, and at the end of twelve hours speech was entirely restored, or, to use Professor Trousseau's emphatic language, "*tout était rentré dans l'ordre.*"*

A striking example of aphasia without paralysis was published by M. Ange Duval in the *Bulletin de la Société de Chirurgie*" for 1864; the subject of it being a lad five years of age, who fell from a window upon his forehead; the result of the fall being a fracture of the frontal bone on the left side. The intelligence of this child continued unaffected, and there was no paralysis, but he never uttered another articulate sound. This boy was accidentally drowned thirteen months after his fall, when an examination of the encephalon disclosed a cyst, of the size of a walnut, which was full of serum, and was evidently the result of a former contusion of the left frontal lobe; this cyst was situated principally in the *third left frontal convolution.*†

Not only does pure uncomplicated aphasia occur, but when loss of speech coincides with hemiplegia, the aphasia may persist after the disappearance of the paralysis. An instance of this was mentioned at the Anatomical Society of Paris by M. Pelvet, who, in exhibiting the brain of a man, aged 56, stated that he

---

* "Clinique Médicale," tom. ij., p. 573.

† The details of this case are given at great length by M. de Font-Réaulx in his thesis for the Doctorate at the Faculty of Medicine of Paris, 1866. It seems that the localization of the faculty of speech has been a subject frequently selected of late for a thesis by graduates of the Paris Faculty. Among the most remarkable, I would mention those of M. de Font-Réaulx and of M. Carrier, both of which have furnished me with interesting matter.

awoke one morning paralysed on the right side of the body, and deprived of the power of speech; the paralysis lasted only two days, but the aphasia persisted.

8.—The defect may be limited to the loss of articulate language only, or may extend to written language, and also to the language of signs. One of these faculties may be destroyed whilst the others remain intact. It would seem that loss of speech more commonly coincides with loss of the power of writing; this, however, is not invariably the case, and Dr. Wm. Ogle has recorded a case of dextral paralysis in which the speech was limited to the two words "yes" and "no," but the power of writing, with the left hand, remained in its integrity. Trousseau records a similar case of a man, who, in coming to consult him, informed him by signs of his inability to speak, but gave him a note, written in a firm hand by himself, in which was contained a detailed account of his disorder; from this note M. Trousseau learned that some days previously he had suddenly lost consciousness, on recovery from which there was no symptom of paralysis, but he found himself unable to articulate a single word.* Dr. Ogle considers that the occasional separation of agraphia and aphasia is an argument in favour of the existence of distinct cerebral centres for the faculties concerned in speaking and writing; while the more frequent coincidence of the two would lead him to infer that these distinct centres must be closely contiguous.† The power both of speaking and writing spontaneously may be suspended, and yet the faculty of imitation may be so well developed

* "Clinique Médicale," tom. j., p. 615.
† St. George's Hosp. Rep., Vol. 2, 1867, p. 100.

that words can be repeated, and even written without difficulty, when they are pronounced by another person.*

In reference to the language of signs and of pantomimic expression, it is more commonly unaffected. In most of the recorded cases the power of communication by signs is not mentioned at all. Lelong, the subject of one of Broca's celebrated cases, could make himself entirely understood by his expressive mimic; I have recorded the same fact in the history of my patient Sainty. Sometimes, pantomimic language, without being abolished, is wanting in precision, or is perverted, as was observed by Dr. Perroud of Lyons, whose patient would make a sign of affirmation when she meant the contrary.† I have lately seen a similar case with my friend Mr. Morgan, in which the signs for assent and dissent were reversed.

Sometimes the faculty of imitation is exaggerated to an extraordinary degree, when the phenomenon is produced which Romberg calls the " echo sign." During a recent visit to La Salpêtrière, Dr. Auguste Voisin kindly called my attention to a remarkable instance of this form then in one of the wards. The subject of it was a woman, aged 56, who had right hemiplegia with aphasia, and who, although she never spoke, repeated all that was said—for instance, Dr. Voisin addressed

---

* Sir Thomas Watson has kindly communicated to me the particulars of a case of dextral paralysis, with not only loss of the power of speaking and writing, but the patient had forgotten her letters, and could not pick out an s or an n in a child's alphabet. This I believe to be an unusual condition, for in most cases the symbol representing a word is recognised when put before the patient; that is when, as in Sir T. Watson's case, the intelligence is unaffected.

† De Font-Réaulx, op. cit. p. 57.

her thus, "Voulez vous manger?" She said, instantly, "Voulez vous manger?" I then said to her, "Quel âge avez vous?" She replied, "Quel âge avez vous?" I then said to her in English, "You are a bad woman." She instantly said, "You are a bad woman." I said, "Sprechen sie Deutsch?" She retorted, "Sprechen sie Deutsch?" In the words that she thus echoed, her articulation was distinct, although the foreign phrases were not repeated by her in quite so intelligible a manner as the French. Not only did this woman echo all that was said, but she imitated every gesture of those around her. One of the pupils made a grimace; she instantly distorted her facial lineaments in precisely the same manner; another pupil made the peculiar defiant action, common in schoolboys, of putting the thumb to the nose and extending all the fingers—called in French, *pied de nez*. The patient instantly imitated this elegant performance. Just as we were leaving her bedside, a patient in an adjoining bed coughed; the cough was instantly imitated by this human parrot! In fact, this singular old woman repeated everything that was said to her, whether in an interrogative form or not; and she imitated every act that was done before her, and that with the most extraordinary exactitude and precision.

Dr. Winslow, under the head of *Morbid Imitation Movements of Articulation*, remarks that he has often observed this echo sign at the commencement of acute attacks of disease of the brain, particularly of inflammatory softening; this condition was observed after death in a case reported by Romberg.*

* "Diseases of the Nervous System," Dr. Sieveking's Translation. Vol. ii., p. 431.

When all other forms of language are either suspended or perverted, there may still remain one, which
is the same in all countries and among all people—the
language of physiognomy : the aphasic may still evince
pleasurable sensations by a smile, give evidence of fear
by pallor of the countenance, and of shame by the blush
on the forehead, " Sæpe tacens vocem, verbaque vultus
habet."*

9.—There is a variety of aphasia characterized by
this peculiarity—that although the subjects of the
affection can articulate nothing else whatever, they can
give vent to an oath, and thus, in the heat of passion or
excitement, words or phrases not always correct as regards taste or ethics are ejaculated, and which the
patient is wholly unable to reproduce when the stimulus
of emotion is wanting.   I have already incidentally
alluded to a case of Dr. Hughlings Jackson, in which
the patient had recovered the power to swear, although
continuing aphasic.   Dr. Gairdner mentions the case of
a patient in the Edinburgh Royal Infirmary whose sole
means of communication with others was by signs.
After a time, Dr. Gairdner noticed that the other
patients believed he was shamming, and on inquiry,
they gave as a reason for their opinion, that he could
swear.   The man shortly afterwards died suddenly,
when his brain was found to be the seat of a large
number of minute deposits of cancer.†

* This language of physiognomy has not been sufficiently considered
by writers on the localisation of the cerebral faculties.   This subject is
fully developed by M. Albert Lemoine in his philosophical treatise
entitled *La Physionomie et la Parole*, Paris, 1865.

† " On the Function of Articulate Speech," p. 14.

Dr. Hughlings Jackson hints that these oaths and interjectional expressions as observed in aphasic patients, may be due to reflex action, and he goes on to say : "It is quite obvious that they are not voluntary, as the patients cannot repeat the phrases. The will cannot act, but somehow an emotion, e.g., anger, gets the words passed through the convolution of language. Just as a paralysed foot will jump up when the sole is tickled, so these words start out when the mind is excited. Such ejaculations seem to have become easy of elaboration by long habit, and require but slight stimulus for perfect execution."*

10.—*Aphasia spasmodica.* Spasmodic mutism occurs in connexion with hysteria and in hypochondriasis, and may be of a more or less persistent character. Dr. Bright has recorded two cases in which the inability to speak coincided with hysterical trismus.† A similar case was lately under my observation, the subject of it being a girl eleven years of age, who, after exposure to cold and damp, was brought to the hospital, because her mother found she was unable to speak. On examining her, it was found that there was a forcible closure of the lower jaw, but the moment the mouth was pressed open, she could speak as before. Dr. Todd, in speaking of an analogous case, uses the word catalepsy in his description of it. Dr. Willis mentions a curious case of this kind, which he calls "paralysis spuria." His description is so quaint that I am tempted to transcribe it :—

* London Hospital Reports, Vol. i., p. 454.
† Bright's Reports of Medical Cases, Vol. ij., part 2., p.p. 459 and 460.

I

"Curo jam nunc fœminam prudentem et probam, quœ per plures annos hujusmodi spuriœ paralysi non tantum in membris sed etiam in linguâ obnoxia fuit; hæc per tempus quoddam libere et expedite satis loquitur, post sermones tamen longos, aut illos festinanter et laboriose prolatos, illico sicut piscis obmutescens, amplius ne *gry* quidem proloqui potest, porro nec nisi post horam unam, aut alteram vocis usuram ullam recuperat."*

Having thus briefly alluded to the principal forms in which loss or lesion of the Faculty of Articulate Language is met with in practice, I propose, in the next place, to consider Aphasia in reference to its Cause, Diagnosis, Prognosis, and Treatment.

* Op. T. Willis, M.D., De Paralysi, De animâ Brutorum, cap. ix., p. 149.

PART V.

Having noticed the different forms in which loss or lesion of the Faculty of Articulate Language is met with by the clinical observer, I now propose to consider the various causes which give rise to this morbid symptom.

The study of the etiology of any disease affords one of the best clues to a clear knowledge of its nature and probable course; and as the pathology of aphasia is involved in so much obscurity, it seems especially desirable carefully to review the various circumstances, physical and moral, under which defects in the power of speech have become developed.

Causes.—A variety of morbid conditions may produce lesion of the faculty of speech.

1°.—It may be congenital as in the deaf and dumb, and it is one of the frequent symptoms of idiocy; the case of G. van A. which I have quoted from Van der Kolk, is a good illustration of this latter condition. The subject of the loquelar defects in idiots is treated in a masterly manner by Dr. Wilbur, Superintendent of the New York State Asylum for Idiots, to whose interesting treatise I would refer for more complete information on this point.*

M. de Font-Réaulx has published the history of a deaf mute, who died at Bicêtre at the age of 60, and at whose autopsy, there was found a remarkable atrophy of the island of Reil on both sides, especially on the left; the brain itself, however, was very large, with its convolutions particularly well developed, the entire encephalon weighing 1,620 grammes (57 ounces).† This observation is of extreme interest as contrasting with the microcephalic brains to which I shall allude hereafter.

The study of the muteness of the deaf is a subject well worthy of the careful investigation of those members of our profession who have the medical charge of institutions for the deaf and dumb, for it is now recognised that this infirmity is partly remediable; in fact, a noted French writer upon this subject says "il est possible de donner la parole à la plus grande partie des sourds-muets, car c'est le plus petit nombre, c'est l'exception qui présente des vices primordiaux ou acquis de l'appareil vocal."‡ In reference to this subject Dr. Gairdner has observed that the aphasic, supposing the disease congenital, could not possibly be educated, but must remain almost an idiot—the mind of an infant enclosed in the shell of a man; he further remarks that in certain forms of cretinism, or of con-

* On Aphasia, New York, 1867.

† Localisation de la faculté spéciale du Langage Articulé, p. 99.

‡ La Surdi-Mutité, par Dr. Blanchet, Chirurgien de l'Institut National des Sourds-Muets, tom. ii., p. 12.

genital idiocy, the primary defect may have been aphasia, and thus the development of the mental faculties an impossibility.*

It has been said that intemperance in one or both parents, about the time of conception, may cause insanity in their offspring; if this be so, it is not unlikely that any morbid cerebral condition of the parents at the period of conception may give rise to aphasia in their children. A case confirmatory of this view has fallen under my own observation, the subject of it being a remarkably fine handsome boy, five years of age, but in whom the faculty of speech could not be roused into action, although he had been submitted to long and special training. Having noticed that he had a well-formed head, that there was no hereditary predisposition to cerebral disease, and that his brothers and sister were by no means backward children, I was induced to push my inquiries very closely in reference to the question of cause; and I then elicited from the father that about ten months previous to the birth of this child, he had been thrown from his horse upon his forehead, that he was stunned by the fall, and that he felt confused in the head for some weeks afterwards. Without wishing to draw any positive conclusion from this case, it seems to me that I am not exceeding the bounds of legitimate inference, in connecting the shock to the nervous system of the father with the congenital defect in the son.

2°.—It may occur as a consequence of direct injury to the brain; of this cause several instances have been

* On the Function of Articulate Speech, p. 32.

given in the preceding pages (Lesur, Castagnon, Romberg, Bergmann, Kolk, H. Jackson). Traumatic cases may be regarded as veritable vivisections, and their study is invaluable in an etiological point of view, as contributing, perhaps more than any other class of cases, to sound ideas as to the question of the cerebral localisation of our divers faculties. Dr. Popham, of Cork, has quoted the following curious case of traumatic aphasia, which is not only interesting from its cause, but from the local morbid condition which coincided with recovery :—A boy, aged 15, received a kick from a cow, between the nose and the forehead, which stunned him, but left apparently at the time, no other injury than a few scratches and slight epistaxis, so that he walked after it some miles to a fair. On the fourth day, he was seized whilst at work with vertigo and loss of speech, his hearing, taste, and sight, as well as deglutition, remaining unaffected. A variety of remedies, amongst others mesmerism, were tried but without any benefit. He continued for twelve months as servant to a medical man, although totally mute, when he got extensive inflammation of the anterior part of the scalp followed by suppuration, and regained his speech as suddenly as he had lost it eighteen or nineteen months before.*

The annals of military surgery are rich in instances of traumatic aphasia the result of gunshot wounds of the head, but the impairment of language is only mentioned as it were *en passant;* now, however, that the attention of the profession is being called to the localisation of the cerebral faculties, it is to be hoped that a more detailed account of the psychological phenomena

* Popham op. cit., p. 9.

attendant on gunshot wounds of the head will in future
be given, and that "*Surgery Militant*" will thus make
its vast resources more available for the settlement of
complex and obscure questions in cerebral pathology.

3°.—Aphasia has frequently been observed as a
symptom of tumours in different parts of the encephalon ;
of sanguineous deposits in the brain and of softening of
that organ; of exostosis or of malformation of the
bones of the cranium ; in fact, of organic lesions of
various kinds affecting the cerebral substance, especially
the anterior lobes.   Instances of loss or impairment of
speech dependent upon each of these causes have been
mentioned in the previous part of this essay.

It would seem that disease in the neighbourhood of
the anterior lobes, but sufficiently near to exercise indirect pressure upon them, may give rise to aphasia.
Dr. A. Voisin has recorded a case where it was caused
by the pressure exercised on the left anterior lobe by a
considerable hæmorrhagic clot in the temporo-sphenoidal
lobe on the same side.*   Dr. Oedmansson, of Stockholm,
mentions a case of tubercles in the brain, in which
aphasia was a symptom during life ; after death there
was found hæmorrhage into the left insula.†

4°.—It may occur as a remote symptom of endo-
pericarditis, where fibrinous vegetations detached from

* Nouveau Dictionnaire de Médecine et de Chirurgie Pratique,
Article Aphasie.

† Dublin Quarterly Journal, Nov. 1868.   Translated from the
Hygiea, by Dr. W. D. Moore. This is a short review of the aphasic
question by a Swedish physician, together with some original cases of
great interest; the author, however, seems but imperfectly acquainted
with the contributions of British authors.

the cardiac valves have been carried into the cerebral arteries (usually the middle cerebral)* and have thus caused embolism; thus establishing a relationship between cardiac disease, obliteration of the middle cerebral artery, softening of the brain from loss of nutrition, and aphasia. As illustrating the above sequence of symptoms, I would refer to the history of William Lemon among my own observations, and to the cases of M. Peter and Dr. Scoresby Jackson, also mentioned in the preceding pages.

The coincidence of cardiac disease with aphasia is most common; it will be remembered that of the thirty-four cases recorded by Dr. Hughlings Jackson in the London Hospital Reports, the heart was more or less affected in twenty instances. Dr. Cesare Lombroso, of Pavia, in commenting upon the cases of Dr. Jackson, denies the construction usually placed on the coincidence of aphasia and disease of the heart and large arteries; according to him, the disease in the nervous centres would be the *cause*, rather than the *consequence*, of the affection of the heart and arteries, the disease in these last depending upon perverted organic nutrition, the result of faulty innervation. Dr. Lombroso further remarks that although there may be cases in which cardiac hypertrophy may determine disorders of the nervous centres, yet, as a rule, these lesions in the circulating organs are secondary and not primary.† Although the high scientific position of the distinguished Italian Professor naturally claims for any statement of his the greatest possible respect, I apprehend that

* We may assume that these vegetations are more likely to pass up the *left* carotid.

† Studi Clinici sulle Malattie Mentali, p. 9.

his views of the sequence of heart and head affections will not be unreservedly adopted by English pathologists.

5°.—It has been observed as a symptom of disease of the spinal cord, (Maty, Abercrombie, &c.); Velpeau, in the Revue Médicale for 1826, has recorded a case of left hemiplegia with aphasia, where after death he found in the centre of the right column of the spinal cord, and in the middle of the cervical portion, a cavity three inches long and two or three lines in diameter, full of soft matter like pus; in the left column of the same portion of the cord, there was a similar disease but to a less extent; the brain was healthy.*

6°.—It may ensue as a nervous symptom; many persons under the influence of anger, joy, or excitement of any kind, are seized with a temporary incapacity to speak. Dr. Todd, under the head of emotional paralysis, mentions the case of a man between fifty and sixty years of age, of an irritable temperament and hypochondriacal habits, who, in a very animated conversation, became excited to such a degree, that his power of speech completely abandoned him; there was no paralysis and the mental faculties were unaffected; he continued speechless, however, for about a week, and in a short time the power of speech fully returned.† Mr. Dunn mentions an instance of aphasia occurring during the latter months of pregnancy, after a sudden and painful shock.‡

* Abercrombie. Diseases of the Brain, p. 357.
† Clinical Lectures on Diseases of the Brain, p. 278.
‡ Medical Psychology, p. 77.

Dr. Panthel, of Limburg, has furnished the following curious illustration of the effect of nervous excitement upon the power of speech.

A peasant boy twelve years of age, previously in good health was very much affected at the grave of his father, whom he had unexpectedly lost. During the interment he threw himself down, and was carried home unconscious. The fainting lasted about a quarter of an hour, when he awoke in the undisturbed possession of all his faculties, sensory and motor, except that he was unable to produce any sound. Dr. Panthel having been summoned, noticed that the intellect was unaffected, that he suffered no pain or uneasiness—as indicated by the motion of the head—but that he had lost his speech and voice, and could utter no sound whatever. He could move the tongue and lips in all possible directions, and the functions of deglutition and respiration were unaffected. On being questioned and urged to speak, he seemed confused, and by a shake of the head expressed his inability. If he attempted to speak, violent spasms were produced in the muscles of the larynx, governed by the hypoglossal nerve—the sterno-thyroid, hyo-thyroid and sterno-hyoid. On Dr. Panthel's compressing these parts with the hand, the cramp immediately ceased, and in answer to the question whether he could speak, he instantly replied, with cheerful countenance: " Yes, speech is my greatest delight!" When the pressure was removed, the inability to speak recurred; the power of utterance being instantly restored by again applying the hand to the supra-laryngeal region. This singular condition lasted three days, when he was again in undisturbed possession of speech. A fortnight afterwards, being in a field, a brace of partridges suddenly flew past him, when the speech defect above described returned for two days. A week later, in consequence of some strong mental emotion, another relapse ensued, which lasted only a few hours. After this no fresh attack occurred, and the lad continued perfectly healthy.*

Instances of suspension of the power of utterance from great mental emotion, are of daily occurrence, and the great writers of antiquity who seem to have been such

* Deutsche Klinik. Jahrgang, 1855. S. 451.

close observers of nature, have not failed to shew their
knowledge of the psychological results of any sudden
and unexpected shock upon the nervous system. Every-
body is familiar with the lines of Virgil in which he
makes Œneas describe the psychical effect produced
upon him by the appearance of the ghost of Creusa :—

> " *Obstupui, steteruntque comœ; vox faucibus hæsit.*"

7°.—The epileptic condition seems to be a frequent
cause of aphasia. Leborgne, Broca's patient, was an
epileptic, as were also the subjects of several of the cases
I have recorded, and the term *epileptic aphemia* has
been applied to them. M. Delasiauve has recorded the
case of an epileptic woman, in whom aphasia alternated
with epilepsy—thus, she would be aphasic for a week,
when on the occurrence of a fit of epilepsy, the power
of speech would return, paralysis of the bladder, however, ensuing ; by and by, she would again lose her
speech and the same sequence of symptoms would
ensue.

A curious instance of the coincidence of aphasia with
epilepsy is recorded by Dr. Oedmansson, where the
epilepsy occurred after a blow on the vertex ; the
aphasia was transient, but frequent ; on every occasion
that several attacks occurred soon after one another, the
power of speech suffered in a greater or less degree,
and was gradually completely lost. When the attacks
ceased or became less frequent, the power of expression
soon returned ; at the same time, both intellectual disturbances and occasionally also paralytic phenomena,
set in and disappeared, but the aphasia always preceded them and was the last to cease.[*]

[*] Oedmansson, op. cit., p. 493.

8°.—It would seem that aphasia is not an uncommon accompaniment of neuralgia and hysteria. At the meeting of the Société Médicale des Hôpitaux, at Paris, April 12, 1867, three cases of loss of speech were mentioned as a symptom or accompaniment of facial neuralgia. The subject of one of them (that mentioned by M. Guyot), was a lady aged 34, who for fourteen years had suffered from facial neuralgia, and who was suddenly seized with aphasia which lasted half an hour and then ceased ; the loss of speech recurred under similar circumstances, when both it and the neuralgia were removed by sulphate of quinine. At a subsequent meeting of the same society, aphasia was spoken of as a frequent accompaniment of hysteria.

Dr. Graves has quoted a case observed by Dr. Richter, of Wiesbaden, of an hysterical female who regularly became speechless every day at four o'clock, p.m. ; consciousness did not appear to be at all impaired, but there was a feeling of weight about the root of the tongue, and the paroxysm went off with a large evacuation of watery urine, accompanied by perspiration and sleep. This periodical aphasia was cured by large doses of quinine.* Another most striking instance of the connexion between loss of speech and hysteria is recorded by Dr. Wells, the subject of it being a woman aged forty-three, who had been subject to fits of an hysterical character for a long time ; on recovery from one of these she found herself entirely deprived of the power of speaking, or even of making any noise whatsoever with her voice, though she was at the same time in full possession of every other faculty, both mental and bodily ; strange to say, her recovery of speech

* Dublin Journal of Medical Science, Jan., 1834, p. 419.

coincided with the occurrence of the next hysterical fit, which took place ten days later.*

"There is," says Dr. Bergmann, "a fixity of thought, as well as a flight of thought, an intellectual catalepsy and chorea." The same may be said of the process by which these thoughts are communicated to the outer world, for it would seem that loss of speech may occur as a cataleptic symptom. Some years since, I attended the widow of an eminent physician, who would sit for hours together with the head forcibly extended on the cervical spine, and who whilst in this position never spoke a word. The intellectual powers of this lady were unimpaired.

9°.—Reflex action. Dr. Brown-Séquard in his course of lectures delivered before the New York Academy of Medicine expressed the opinion that aphasia was a reflex phenomenon. Sauvages, under the name of *Mutitas Verminosa*, mentions the case of a child in whom loss of speech was due to the presence of worms; anthelmintics having been administered, thirty-six lumbrici were expelled, when speech was restored with the exception of a difficulty in pronouncing the letter B.†

Hoffmann also mentions a similar case where the cerebral irritation from reflex action was more permanent and accompanied by opisthotonos. The occurrence of the aphasia was sudden, but although the administration of anthelmintics soon resulted in the expulsion of fifteen worms, it was only after an appropriate treatment of many weeks that the power of speech began to

* Medical Communications, Vol. 2, p., 501. London, 1790.
† Nosologia Methodica, tom. i., p. 779.

improve.* The same author says elsewhere that he has frequently seen and cured cases of loss of speech from the presence of worms.

Dr. Gibson, of Hull, has also recorded a case of aphasia with complete paralysis of the extremities, caused by Trichocephalus dispar, and cured in twelve days by appropriate treatment.†

10°.—Several instances are on record in which loss of speech supervened on atmospheric changes, or on application of cold or heat to the head. In the case I have quoted from Dr. Jackson, of Pennsylvania, the aphasia occurred after a check to the cutaneous perspiration from exposure to the night air; Dr. Banks records an instance of aphasia and deafness occurring after fatigue on a *very cold day*; and Abercrombie mentions a case of a young man who bathed twice in the river Tweed, and who after coming out the second time lay down on the bank and fell asleep without his hat, exposed to the intense heat of the sun. On awaking he was *speechless*, but walked home, and seemed to be otherwise in good health.‡

Ten years ago an invalid soldier came under my own observation, who five months previously, whilst at Corfu, had a *sunstroke* which caused left hemiplegia and *loss of speech for a week*. This case is of some interest, not only from the paralysis being on the *left* side, but also from my having made a note of it long before I could have had any preconceived ideas about modern localisation theories.

* Hoffmanni Opera, tom. iii., cap. vii., obs. iii.
† Lancet, Aug. 9, 1862.
‡ Abercrombie, op. cit. p. 155.

11°.—Certain drugs, especially those obtained from the Natural Order Solanaceæ, would seem in some instances to suspend the power of speech. Sauvages, under the head of *Mutitas a narcoticis*, says that certain robbers which infested the neighbourhood of Montpellier, in order the more successfully to exercise their profession, were in the habit of drugging wine with the seeds of the Datura Stramonium, the effect of which was, that those who drank it could not speak for one or two days, although wide awake. He also states that he has observed the same effect from the berries of the Atropa Belladonna and from the roots of Hyoscyamus Niger. This shrewd observer has not omitted to speak of that want of control over speech produced by alcohol "*idem accidit cum temulentiâ imò a vini abusu balbuties orta quotidie observatur.*"*

Dr. Paget Blake, of Torquay, has published a case of poisoning by Stramonium (1½ drachm of the tincture), in which the patient on recovering his speech—which he had at first entirely lost—misnamed almost everything he wanted, although he was evidently quite unaware that he did so; several days elapsed ere he could mention his wants without calling something by a wrong name.† It will be observed that the aphasia, which was *atactic* at first, before passing off assumed the *amnesic* form. Dr. Popham, of Cork, has noticed the occurrence of temporary dumbness in a boy who had eaten the roots of "Œnanthe Crocata" which he had mistaken for field carrots.‡

* Nosologia Methodica, tom. i., p. 177.

† St. George's Hospital Reports, 1868, p. 159, where minute details of this interesting case are given.

‡ Dublin Quarterly Journal of Medical Science, Nov., 1865, p. 484.

Dr. Nichols, of Chelmsford, reports that he has seen aphasia produced by the administration of Cannabis Indica, and Dr. John Ogle has recorded a case, in which opium given in small doses always caused the patient to be talkative, "to talk foolishly," as she called things by their wrong names; the peculiarity passed off when the effects of the drug ceased. There was no symptom whatever of any cerebral disease, and Dr. Ogle presumes that the effect of the opium was the result of some peculiar modification of the cellular or vascular action within the brain.*

12°.—Septicæmia. Blood poisoning—whether from uræmia as in Bright's disease, or from alcoholism, gout, plumbism, or syphilis—is another frequent cause, illustrations having been furnished by Andral, Jaccoud, Heymann, and Auguste Voisin. The case of Anna Maria Moore reported by myself, may be considered as due to blood poisoning, for a diseased action which is set down as the result of the climacteric change, may be due to the retention in the system of certain morbid and effete matters—some irritating compound in the blood—which ought to be eliminated by the kidneys, and thus a septicæmic condition is produced.

Hoffmann mentions the case of a girl of eighteen, who, on exposure to cold during a journey at the period of menstruation, was seized with symptoms of cerebral congestion, and was dumb for four days, the mind and senses remaining unaffected; after an evacuant and diaphoretic treatment she entirely recovered.†

* Lancet, Aug. 22, 1868.

† Op. citato, tom. iii., cap. vii., obs. i.

The suspension more or less complete of the power of speech which sometimes occurs after continued fever, is probably due to a vitiated condition of the blood circulating through the brain. It occurs more frequently after enteric than typhus fever; Dr. S. Jackson, however, mentions three cases in which typhus coincided with impaired speech;* Dr. Osborne has recorded three instances of gastro-enteric fever, in which loss of speech occurred without disturbance of the intellect; and Trousseau mentions three cases, one observed by himself, and two by M. Boucher, of Dijon, in which aphasia occurred during *convalescence* from fever (dothinenterie); in two of these cases there was albumen in the urine.†
In a case recorded by M. Augier, the aphasic symptoms seem to have been due to a cerebro-meningeal hyperæmia, caused by the excessive use of cider in a person who in early youth had been a great brandy drinker.‡

In the category of causes we are now considering must be classed the poison introduced into the system by the bite of venomous snakes. M. Ruftz stated at a meeting of the Paris Anthropological Society, that he had seen a certain number of persons who had completely lost their speech in consequence of a bite from a serpent (Fer de lance); sometimes aphasia was produced instantly, and at other times, some hours only after the bite; but, what was most remarkable, those who survived the poisoning remained permanently aphasic. Van der Kolk quotes the case of a gunner in the Dutch Indies, who was bitten by a serpent called by the natives, Oeloer; in a few minutes he became

* "Edinburgh Medical Journal," Jan., 1847.
† Clinique Médicale, tom. iii., p. 618.
‡ Gazette des Hôpitaux, March 8, 1866.

K

giddy and lost the power of swallowing; *there was total loss of speech*, but consciousness was unimpaired; death occurred four hours and a half after receipt of the injury.*

I have dwelt thus upon blood-poisoning as a cause of impairment of speech, because it seems to me to have an important bearing on the question of localisation of the faculty of articulate language; for since in our days *humourism* has given way to *solidism*, there is a tendency to connect all abnormal cerebral symptoms with change of tissue, whereas, temporary loss of speech, at all events, does not necessarily require for its production positive lesion of brain substance, any more than jaundice from obstruction and reabsorption of bile, need in all cases imply structural disease of the liver.

DIAGNOSIS.—Having in this essay employed the word aphasia in its widest and most general sense, as applicable to loss of speech from whatsoever cause, the existence of this defect is so easy of recognition, that but little need be said under the head of diagnosis; although as regards the various forms which this defect assumes, and the pathological conditions which give rise to them, the *differential diagnosis* becomes important.

I need scarcely observe that aphasia must not be confounded with aphonia, where the voice is only suppressed, but the faculty of speech remains. Although it has been stated that this distinction was not observed by the older authors, still, from a careful study of their works, it will be seen that in many instances the confusion was only apparent, and depended on the use of

* Dr. W. D. Moore's Translation, p. 162.

a faulty nomenclature; for it is evident that the authors themselves were fully aware of the wide difference between these two morbid conditions.*

In the form of paralysis recently described by Trousseau, under the name of *Labio-glosso-laryngeal Paralysis*, there is no impairment of the faculty of speech; it is simply a mechanical defect dependant on paralysis of the tongue, lips, and of the muscles of the larynx. Aphasia may be apparent only, instances having occurred in the Essex Hall Idiot Asylum, where children who for many years had passed for deaf and dumb, unexpectedly gave evidence of the possession of the power of speech. One boy, supposed to be a deaf-mute, was heard one night to sing a chant which had been used at public worship, pronouncing the words distinctly, and giving the tune correctly. Another boy, also passing for a deaf-mute, broke into a violent passion in consequence of something on his slate being rubbed out, and demanded of another lad why he had done it.

In an obscure subject like this we cannot afford to dispense with any of the auxiliary aids to differential diagnosis. With the view, therefore, of determining whether loss of speech depended in any particular case on softening, or whether it was the result of mechanical pressure exercised by a clot or by some morbid growth, it has occurred to me to make a volumetric analysis of the urine, upon the assumption that in cases of soften-

* Hoffmann uses the word aphonia in the description of his cases as does also Mr. Carmichael Smith, in his extremely interesting paper in the Medical Communications for 1790; but it will be seen from a perusal of their clinical histories, that the authors intended to describe instances of inability to articulate.

ing there would be more disintegration of nervous tissue, and consequently an excess of phosphorus removed from the system.*

On referring to those among my own cases where a quantitative analysis of the urine was made, it will be observed that the results were negative, inasmuch as there was no deviation from the ordinary range, except in one instance—that of the patient Sainty—when the amount of chlorides was 10 parts per 1,000, the ordinary range being, according to Beale, from 4 to 8 parts per 1000.

Although my own experiments in reference to the urine cannot be considered as in any way conclusive— being based on too small a number of cases—I cannot but think, however, that a quantitative as well as a qualitative analysis of the urine is imperatively called for in all cases of obscure cerebral disease ; and since the introduction of the volumetric system, this analysis has become much easier of accomplishment, and ought never to be omitted where the least doubt exists as to exact diagnosis. "How many cases," says Todd, "formerly supposed to be anomalous, are now readily understood by reference to uræmic poisoning through inefficient kidneys.†

* I am by no means prepared to say that this assumption is absolutely correct, but whether it be so or not, inquiries in this direction cannot be otherwise than useful.

† Dr. Todd further remarks that there are many other points of interest in connection with the state of the urine in brain disease, which can only be settled by many observers, such as the variations of the phosphates, the quantity of the sulphates and the chlorides, and whether, in the marked increase or decrease of these salts or elements of the urinary secretion, we can derive any trustworthy aid to determine the inflammatory or non-inflammatory nature of the brain lesion.— Clinical Lectures on Diseases of the Brain, p. 311.

The Sphygmograph may render essential service in affording a clue to the probable condition of the arteries of the brain, and thus enable us to form an opinion as to whether aphasic symptoms are due to structural or merely functional disease. Dr. Sansom has kindly communicated to me the particulars of a case of aphasia, in which Dr. Anstie, on applying the sphygmograph, noticed a decrease of arterial tone, and that there was a decided difference between the two sides.*

Thermometric observation may be of assistance in the clinical recognition of the morbid lesion giving rise to the aphasic symptoms. The result of Professor Broca's observations on aphasic patients has been to show *an elevation of temperature above the left ear*, in those who are the subjects of cerebral softening. According to the distinguished Parisian Professor, the increase is sometimes two or three degrees centigrade, and in that case it can be appreciated by the hand; when the rise in the temperature is less, the variation can only be recognised by the aid of the thermometer. M. Broca thinks that when aphasia is the result of *progressive atrophy of the third frontal convolution*, there is probably a decrease, instead of a rise of temperature, but this fact he has not yet verified.†

* It is to be hoped that Dr. Sansom will be induced to publish this most interesting case *in extenso*.

† M. Broca's method of taking the temperature in these cases is as follows :—He takes two perfectly similar thermometers, covers them with little bags of wadding, and then applies them on each side of the head, fixing them by means of a circular band. It is essential that the two little bags should be of the same thickness, weight, and form. At the end of ten minutes he reads off the position of the mercury, and marks the difference.

PROGNOSIS.—Some authorities have considered sudden loss of speech as necessarily indicative of grave cerebral disorder. Dr. Winslow says it is most unusual for sudden speechlessness to exist without being immediately followed by acute cerebral symptoms. Dr. Copland seems to share the same opinion, for in his work on Palsy and Apoplexy, he says that "loss of the power of articulation, except in hysterical cases, is either attendant on, or followed by, the most complete or fatal states of palsy or apoplexy." Trousseau also considers the aphasia which is accompanied by hemiplegia, of the most serious import, and alludes to its frequent termination by "*apoplexie foudroyante*," giving three instances in which this fatal result ensued.*

A glance at the observations which I have recorded in the preceding pages, will shew that loss of speech, although often of ominous and serious portent, is not unfrequently perfectly amenable to treatment, the function being sometimes completely restored in a very short time. The Prognosis, however, must necessarily depend on the cause which has given rise to the symptom; when it occurs as a sequel of continued fever, when it occurs as a neurosis, or is of hysterical origin, or when it arises from any moral cause, a recovery may be anticipated. The chances of the complete restoration of the faculty are also much greater when the aphasia is simple and uncomplicated with any paralytic symptom. When hemiplegia coexists with aphasia, the return of motor power usually coincides with a corresponding improvement in speech; this, however, is not always the case, as for instance in the observation of Sir Thomas Watson, to which I have already alluded,

* Clinique Médicale, tom. ii., p. 625.

where, although the paralysis disappeared, there was no corresponding amelioration in the power of articulation.*

TREATMENT.—Having admitted that aphasia is only a symptom, and not a disease of itself, its treatment must obviously depend upon the cause which produces it. Still, some practical good may result from a brief consideration of the mode of treatment applicable to the various forms of loss or lesion of speech which are observed in practice; and at the same time the pathology of this obscure symptom may perhaps receive some elucidation from a brief analysis of the therapeutical measures, which have been more or less successfully adopted in the numerous cases which have now been submitted to the profession.

In those cases that are associated with hemiplegia, and where there is structural disease to account for it, there can be no special treatment for the aphasic complication; but in those instances where loss of speech is the sole or principal symptom, medical science may do something toward removing the morbid condition.

In those cases which seem to depend on the circulation of some morbid product through the brain, whether from faulty kidneys or sluggishness of other secreting

---

* In reference to the persistence of amnesic aphasia after the disappearance of all other morbid cerebral symptoms, Van Swieten has the following passage :—"Vidi plures, qui ab apoplexia curati omnibus functionibus cerebri recte valebant nisi quod deesset hoc unicum, quod non possent vera rebus designandis vocabula invenire; manibus, pedibus, totius corporis nixu conabantur explicare miseri, quid vellent, nec poterant tamen. Malum illud per plures annos sæpe insanabile perstat."—*Van Swieten Commentaria in Boerhaave*, tom. iii. §1018.

organs, a treatment actively eliminatory will be found beneficial. Long before the attention of the profession was specially called to the lesion of articulate language, a remarkable instance of recovery of the power of speech after free purging, which brought away several fetid, dark-coloured stools, was observed by Dr. Richard Jones.* A French physician, M. Mattei, has seen aphasia the consequence of constipation entirely removed by repeated injections; after giving minute details of this case, which is full of interest, he says, "*La malade a rempli en une demi-heure trois énormes vases de matières fécales, et lorsque l'intestin à été tout à fait vidé, la parole est devenue aussi précise que si la femme n'avait rien eu.*"†

As far back as 1790, Dr. J. Carmichael Smith has recorded a case of loss of speech of some months' duration, which yielded to an emetic.‡

Surely the successful treatment of such cases as the above is very significative in reference to the question of localisation, and must be a source of difficulty to those who adhere to the doctrine of a separate and limited centre for speech.

Venesection or abstraction of blood by leeching or cupping may occasionally be useful where the morbid condition is dependent on temporary congestion; in the case of Professor Rostan, as well as in that I have quoted from Dr. Jackson, of Pennsylvania, speech was rapidly restored by the abstraction of a little blood.

* Edinburgh Medical Journal, 1809, p. 281.

† Gazette des Hôpitaux, June 15, 1865.

‡ Medical Communications, Vol. II., p. 488. London, 1790. The particulars of this case are of extreme interest, as also those of two others described in the same communication.

When we have reason to infer that the brain lesion is of an irritative character—as perhaps indicated by early rigidity of the paralysed muscles, and by their extreme sensibility to the galvanic stimulus—we are justified in expecting some benefit from the abstraction of blood; where an opposite condition exists, bleeding will probably be worse than useless.

When loss of speech occurs in hysterical and highly excitable persons, or is an accompaniment of the choreic or epileptic condition and may depend on a spasmodic state of the cerebral arteries, diffusive stimulants and antispasmodics will be found of service. Crichton mentions a case in which large doses of Valerian were effectual, and Dr. Hutchison, of the United States, has recorded a case where hysterical loss of speech was cured by Etherisation.*

There are certain cases in which the aphasia seems to depend on a kind of cerebral catalepsy, and where very powerful stimulants, such as electricity, prove of great value. I have elsewhere stated that in one of my own cases, that of Sutherland, electricity had a decidedly baneful effect; and in this affection, as well as in motor paralysis, this powerful remedial agent must be used with the greatest caution. In reference to its use, we cannot do better than observe the distinction laid down by Dr. Todd—that electricity is injurious when there is an early tendency to muscular rigidity, showing an exalted polarity of nervous tissue, and probably an irritating lesion of the brain; thus, when the aphasia is an accompaniment of muscular paralysis, the result of electricity on the limbs affected may serve to guide

* Medical Times, July 29th, 1865.

us in our diagnosis, by showing whether the lesion is irritative or depressing.*

Strong mental emotion is often salutary in such cases; we are all familiar with the story in Herodotus of the son of Crœsus, who had never been known to speak, but who, at the siege of Sardis, being overcome with astonishment and terror at seeing the king—his father —in danger of being killed by a Persian soldier, exclaimed aloud—Ανθρωπε μὴ κτείνε Κρôισον—Oh, man, do not kill Crœsus! This was the first time he had ever articulated, but he retained the faculty of speech from this event as long as he lived.† Herodotus is universally admitted to be a trustworthy historian, but if it be thought far-fetched to illustrate a subject by allusion to a work written 500 years before the Christian era, I may add that such cases have been met with by other observers. My friend, Mr. Dunn, has recorded a similar one, and a few months ago, I myself was invited

* In the "Lancet," for January 23rd, 1869, Dr. Marcet has mentioned a most striking instance of the benefit of electricity in a case of hemiplegia with aphasia, where, after recovery from the paralysis, the loss of speech continued. Dr. Marcet, having determined to try galvanism with Smee's battery, one of the electrodes was applied, by means of Mackenzie's galvaniser, to the tongue, and the other to the back of the neck, in contact with the spine. Speech began to return from the very first application of the galvanism, and continued steadily to improve each time it was used.

† Herod. Hist. I., 85. Aulus Gellius, after repeating the above story from Herodotus, relates a similar fact in the following terms :—Sed et quispiam Samius athleta, nomen illi fuit Αἰγλῆς, quum antea non loquens fuisset, ob similem dicitur causam loqui cœpisse. Nam quum in sacro certamine sortitio inter ipsos et adversarios non bona fide fieret, et sortem nominis falsam subjici animadvertisset, repente in eum, qui id faciebat, sese videre, quid faceret, magnum inclamavit. Atque is oris vinculo solutus, per omne inde vitæ tempus, non turbidè neque adhæsè locutus est. *Noctes Atticœ. lib.* V. *cap.* ix.

by Mr. Allen, of Norwich, to see with him a man, aged 37, who had been in his usual health up to the day preceding my visit, when, during a meal, his wife noticed that all his limbs were shaking, and from this time he became speechless. The suspension of speech was unaccompanied by any symptom of paralysis, and the loss of the faculty of articulate language continued for six days, when being asleep on his couch, he suddenly started up, and was heard to say three times, "*A man in the river!*" From this moment speech was restored, and when I saw him an hour afterwards, he told me that he had dreamed that a man was falling into the river; the mental shock produced by this dream was salutary, for it resuscitated the previously dormant faculty of articulate language.

In our efforts at the restoration of speech, we must not lose sight of the fact that as muscles from want of use lose their contractile power, and become atrophied, so it is possible that the convolution or portion of brain presiding over articulate language—assuming *pro hâc vice* that there is such a localised centre—may, from long disuse and actual cessation of function, undergo a change of some kind, by which the patient may be somewhat in the same condition as that of a child who has not yet learned to speak; thus, one of the most interesting features in the treatment of certain cases of aphasia is the education of the organs of the speech, as it were, *de novo*.

Several instances has been recorded confirmatory of this view. M. Piorry relates the history of a merchant who had to re-learn his a b c.* Dr. Banks' case of the

* Gazette des Hôpitaux, May 27, 1865.

gentleman re-learning Greek and Latin is a further illustration, as also the remarkable observation of Dr. Hun, which I have recorded when treating of the American contributions to this subject.* Perhaps the most satisfactory result of efforts to re-learn to speak is that recorded by Dr. Osborne, in connexion with his remarkable case to which I have already alluded under the head of *Varieties*. Dr. Osborne says :—"Having explained to the patient my view of the peculiar nature of his case, and having produced a complete conviction in his mind that the defect lay in his having lost, not the power, but the art, of using the vocal organs, I advised him to commence learning to speak like a child, repeating first the letters of the alphabet, and subsequently words after another person. The result has been most satisfactory, and affords the highest encouragement to those who may labour under this peculiar kind of deprivation ; there being now very little doubt, if his health is spared, and his perseverance continues, that he will obtain a perfect recovery of speech."†

However hypothetical, therefore, the re-education of the nervous centres may, at first sight, appear, there exists sufficient evidence to induce us, in all cases where cerebral loss of speech is unattended by any marked lesion of the intelligence, to endeavour gradually to rouse into action the complex apparatus, the concurrence of which is necessary for the re-establishment of man's noblest prerogative—the faculty of articulate language.

---

* Vide Journal of Mental Science, April, 1868.
† Dublin Journal of Medical Science, Nov., 1833, p. 169.

PART VI

In the first two parts of this essay I entered into the subject of the bibliography of aphasia, as illustrated by the French, German, Dutch, British, and American writers; the third part contains a detailed account of the clinical history of cases that have fallen under my own immediate observation; the fourth treats of the different forms and varieties in which loss or lesion of articulate language is met with in practice; whilst in the fifth part, I have considered the subject in reference to the question of Cause, Diagnosis, Prognosis, and Treatment.

We are now, therefore, in a position to criticise the value of the different opinions which have been pro- pounded as to the precise point of the cerebro-spinal centre which is affected in aphasia, or in other words, to consider whether there be a cerebral seat of speech at all, and if so, where it is located; and I propose in this concluding part to summarise, and carefully to weigh the evidence furnished by the numerous cases recorded in the previous pages. Leaving for the present the question of the existence or non-existence of a speech centre, and assuming *pro hâc vice* that there is one, I shall proceed at once to consider the different theories which have been from time to time promulgated as to the seat of articulate language.

The ancients seemed to have possessed the most crude notions of the functions of the brain, as evidenced by Hippocrates assigning the seat of the mind to the left ventricle, and by Aristotle also placing the sensorium commune in the heart; Michael Servetus, who flourished in the sixteenth century, believed the choroid plexus was the organ destined to secrete the animal spirits, that the fourth ventricle was the seat of memory, and that the habitation of the soul was in the aqueduct of Sylvius; a century later, René Descartes assigned to the soul a more secure position in the pineal gland. In later times, the brain has been universally considered to be the organ of thought and intelligence, but opinions have been and are still divided, as to whether it is to be regarded as a single organ, or as consisting of a series of distinct organs, each endowed with a special and independent function—whether, in fact, the phenomena of intelligence are due to an action of the brain as a whole, or whether the different psychological elements which constitute them are connected with isolated and circumscribed parts of the encephalon.*

Out of the last theory has arisen the principle of the localisation of the cerebral faculties, which was first announced in a definite form by Gall, who divided the encephalon into organs endowed with primordial faculties, distinct the one from the others. The germ of this

---

* Those who may desire more detailed information as to the various theories of the seat of speech which were in vogue before the time of Gall, I would refer to an extremely interesting series of papers recently published by the late Dr. Hunt in the Anthropological Review.

idea of the polysection of the encephalon is to be found in the writings of physiologists long before the time of Gall; indeed, one writer, Charles Bonnet, assigned a special function to each fibre, stating that every faculty, sensitive, moral, or intellectual, was in the brain connected to a bundle of fibres, that every faculty had its own laws which subordinated it to other faculties, and determined its mode of action, and that not only had every faculty its fasciculus of fibres, but that every word had its own fibre!

The circumstance which directed Gall's attention to the possibility of connecting the brain with certain faculties of our mental nature is so well known that I scarcely need allude to it. In his early days, he often found himself surpassed by certain of his fellow students whom he felt were intellectually inferior to himself, but in whom a remarkable memory coincided with a striking prominence of the ocular globes. This external prominence led him to the inference that there was an internal cerebral prominence which produced it, and it was the application of this reasoning to other cranial protuberances that gave rise to his craniological doctrine.

According to Gall, the brain is composed of various parts, to each of which a special function belongs, and his system embraces the topographical determination of each of these organs. The organs of the memory of words, of the memory of persons, and of the faculty of language, he located in the convolutions which rest on the floor of the orbit, and which form the inferior surface of the anterior lobe; the organ of the memory of persons he placed immediately above the inner angle of the orbit, that of the memory words in the convolution which rests on the posterior half of the roof of the orbit, whilst the organ of language or speech he placed in the convolution which rests on the anterior half of the orbital roof, in front of the preceding faculty.

The minute anatomy of the convolutions was unknown in the time of Gall, and he based his phrenological theories rather on the external prominences of the skull—on cranioscopy—than upon a careful study of the convolutions to which these prominences corresponded, and although his conclusions must be considered in many instances arbitrary and hypothetical, still I would say "Let not the spark be lost in the flame it has served to kindle," for in spite of all that has been said against Gall, and all that has been written in depreciation of his labours, beyond all doubt, his researches gave an impulse to the cerebral localisation of our faculties, the effect of which is especially visible in our own days; and I look upon his work as a vast storehouse of knowledge, and as an imperishable monument to the genius and industry of one of the greatest philosophers of the present age.*

* Gall's labours would undoubtedly have met with a more hearty recognition from his contemporaries, had not the Austrian priesthood raised the cry of "materialism" as applied to his doctrines. The great German psychologist had no such heterodox notions as his adversaries maliciously attributed to him, for as Hufeland philosophically observes, "he was employed in analysing the dust of the earth of which man is formed, not the breath of life which was breathed into his nostrils."

As in Gall's days so in ours, this very indefinite and unmeaning word "materialism" is used as a kind of psychological scare-crow to frighten all those who are endeavouring to trace the connexion between matter and mind. Surely there is nothing contrary to sound theology in assigning certain attributes or functions of an intellectual order to certain parts of our nervous centre; the cerebral localisation of our divers faculties, and the plurality of our cerebral organs, strike no blow at the great principle of the moral unity of man. The same

Gall's conclusions were based purely on the study of anatomy, but subsequent observers — Bouillaud, Schroeder Van Der Kolk, and Broca—have brought the light of pathological observation to shine upon this obscure subject, and, with the view of testing the soundness of the respective theories advanced by these physiologists, I propose briefly to weigh the evidence which has been furnished for or against the four different theories which have, in modern times, been promulgated as to the seat of speech; and here I would observe, that this question will never be settled by mere theoretical speculation, without the aid of that inexorable scrutiniser of facts—necroscopic examination.

I will first discuss the theory which has perhaps found the fewest advocates—that of Schroeder Van Der Kolk—who placed the seat of speech in the corpora olivaria, a theory which has lately found a warm supporter in M. Jaccoud, who thus expresses himself in reference to it;—"The functional centre of the articulation of sounds and of deglutition is situated in the medulla oblongata. It is constituted respectively by the union of the hypoglossal, the facial, the glossopharyngeal, the spinal accessory, and the trifacial nerves. For the isolated movements of the tongue, of the lips, of the cheeks, of the velum palati, and of the pharynx, each of these nerves acts independently in its sphere of distribution; but for the complex and simultaneous

power that caused the earth "like a spark from the incandescent mass of unformed matter, hammered from the anvil of omnipotence, to be smitten off into space," this same power, surely, could just as well ordain that a multiplicity of organs should be necessary to the full development of man's mental faculties, as that the manifestation of them should depend upon the integrity of one single organ.

L

movements which are necessary for the production of
articulate sounds and of deglutition, all the original
nuclei of these nerves are connected together, also the one
side with the other, by the olivary system, which thus
becomes the co-ordinating organ of the final functional
act."* A more recent writer, M. Vulpian, criticises
most severely Van Der Kolk's conclusions, and quotes
a case observed by himself, where, although the olivary
bodies were both manifestly diseased, yet speech remained perfectly unimpaired to the last.†

Of the sixty-three cases to which I have called attention in the preceding pages, I find that in five only the
olivary bodies were stated as having been found diseased
after death. The first three cases are quoted by Van
Der Kolk. In one of these, in addition to atrophy of
the olivary bodies, there was an extremely imperfect
development of the frontal convolutions, and also a
positively diseased condition of the anterior lobes; in
another case, although there was found grey degeneration of the right olivary body, there was also disease of
other parts, namely, in the crura cerebri, the corpus
callosum, one of the thalami, the fornix, and the corpora pyramidalia; in the third case I have quoted from
Van Der Kolk, as well as in one from Abercrombie, in
addition to the disease in the corpora olivaria, there
was also disease in one of the crura cerebelli and in the
tubercula mamillaria; and, lastly, in a case observed
by Romberg, the affection of the corpus olivare coincided with disease in the right half of the pons Varolii.
It must, therefore, be conceded, that as in all these

* Gazette Hebdomadaire de Médecine et de Chirurgie, July 22, 1864.

† Leçons sur la Physiologie générale et comparée du Système
Nerveux, p. 495.

cases, in addition to a diseased state of the olivary bodies, there was extensive disease in other parts, they cannot be looked upon as substantial evidence in favour of the localisation of speech in the corpora olivaria; in fact, Cruveilhier, who was the author of all the cases which I have quoted from Van Der Kolk's work, was quite innocent himself of drawing from them any inference as to the connexion of the olivary bodies with the articulation of words.*

The next theory for consideration is that of M. Bouillaud, who places the seat of speech in the anterior lobes, and who, twenty years ago, offered a prize of 500 francs for any well authenticated case negativing his views. Although this theory has met with less opposition than the others, several cases have been recorded, which, to say the least, throw considerable doubt upon its truth. Let us see what evidence the previous pages of this essay furnish for or against the views of M. Bouillaud, who, it must be remembered, admits that speech may exist with one frontal lobe destroyed, but who maintains that when both are destroyed or seriously damaged, articulate language becomes impossible.

* Since the above was penned, my attention has been called to the latest publication on the anatomy of the medulla oblongata in this country, in which the author, Dr. Lockhart Clarke, mentions two cases of aphasia, in each of which one of the olivary bodies was diseased, being in the one case atrophied, and in the other the seat of a former clot. In both these instances there were numerous and extensive lesions in other parts of the brain, therefore—as Dr. Clarke also admits —they by no means prove that the loss of speech was due to the diseased condition of the olivary bodies.—"Researches on the Intimate Structure of the Brain." Philosophical Transactions 1868, Pt. I., p. 312.

I have quoted three cases* in which both anterior lobes were destroyed or very extensively injured. What does a conscientious analysis of them teach us? In M. Peter's case we have seen that speech was preserved, although both frontal lobes were reduced to a pulp (réduits en bouillie); in one of M. Trousseau's cases, a ball had traversed the two frontal lobes at their centre, entering at one temple and making its exit by the other, articulation remaining unimpaired during the six months the patient survived this fearful injury; in M. Velpeau's celebrated case a scirrhous tumour had replaced the two anterior lobes; but instead of being speechless the man was remarkably loquacious.†

These three cases, to which I could add others, seem to upset M. Bouillaud's doctrine by showing that a profound lesion may exist in both anterior lobes, without impairment of articulate language; but on the other hand, it is only fair to observe that in none of them was there positive evidence of the complete destruction of the anterior lobes, for in M. Peter's case, although the lesion must have been extensive, still, as the words "*cornes frontales*" are used to describe the

---

* *Vide* Part I., pp. 14, 18, 19.

† It is well known that tumours of the brain, by their slow and gradual development, frequently compress, deform, and displace the cerebral tissue, without sensibly altering the function of that organ; and it has been suggested, that in these cases there may be a sort of unfolding of the brain tissue by the pressure of the tumour which has developed itself in its place, but not at the expense of the tissue itself, which, in its new relations, and under the form and volume to which it has been reduced, may still retain the integrity of its structure, and its habitual functional aptitude. I need scarcely add, that this explanation cannot apply to the cases I have quoted, in which integrity of speech coincided with tumours involving nearly the entire anterior lobe.

part injured, the posterior part of the same lobes may possibly have remained unaffected; again, in M. Trousseau's case it is possible to conceive that the transit of a ball through both anterior lobes may have left a portion of the cerebral substance uninjured; in reference to M. Velpeau's barber, in reading carefully the details of the autopsy as noted in the Bulletins de l'Académie de Médecine, I find it stated that a portion of the right anterior lobe was not involved in the tumour, also that at the posterior, external, and inferior part of the left lobe, there was a certain thickness of cerebral substance unimpaired.

The adversaries of the localisation of speech in the anterior lobes have attached an immense importance to a case mentioned by Cruveilhier of a congenital idiot, who could pronounce words distinctly articulated, although after death it was found that there was congenital absence of the two anterior lobes. This observation has such an important bearing upon our present inquiry, that an abridgement of it must find a place here.

Alexandrine Vaillosge, a congenital idiot, came under observation at the age of twelve—the idiocy being carried to the highest degree. She could neither dress nor feed herself; although she could move her limbs in all directions, she was unable to co-ordinate her movements for the act of walking, and it was necessary to carry her from place to place. The sense of smell seemed not to exist, or rather the young idiot was insensible to bad odours; the other senses presented nothing remarkable. If one threatened to strike her she would make the most frightful noises. The desire for food was readily felt, and when hungry she would express her wants by means of words *very distinctly articulated*. This girl having died at the age of fifteen of chronic diarrhœa, the following post-mortem appearances were observed :—The skull was very well formed exteriorly, but its cavity was not completely filled by the brain. The anterior lobes were entirely absent, and a limpid serum contained in the cavity of the arachnoid occupied the space which separated the anterior extremity of the brain from the frontal portion of the dura mater. Strange to say, the orbital plates, although not in contact with the brain, but with serum, presented the mammillary eminences and digital impressions exactly similar to those of a healthy individual of the same age. With the exception of the absence of the anterior lobe, the left hemisphere completely filled the corresponding part of the skull; the right hemisphere, the size of which was only about half that of the left, was separated from the parietes of the skull by a space filled with serum.*

Cruveilhier himself seems to have considered this case as fatal to the doctrine of the localisation of speech in the anterior lobes; on examining, however, carefully the beautiful plate annexed to the description of this case, it is evident that when the author stated that the two anterior lobes were wanting, he did not limit these lobes in the same way that we do now. For Cruveilhier, the anterior lobes were limited inferiorly to that part of the hemisphere which lies on the root of the orbit,† for a glance at the plate will show that only the anterior half of the left frontal lobe was destroyed; the transverse frontal convolution was preserved, as well as the posterior half of the 1st, 2nd, and 3rd frontal convolutions; although the disease in the right hemisphere was more extensive, still the plate shows that a considerable portion of it still remained. According, therefore, to our present mode of dividing the brain, this case cannot be cited as impugning M. Bouillaud's theory.

* Cruveilhier, Anatomie Pathologique, 8° Livraison, pl. 6.

† This limitation of the anterior lobe is correct only as far as the orbital convolutions are concerned, for a glance at the plate, forming frontispiece to this essay, will show that above the orbital portion the anterior lobe extends very much further backwards.

I now pass to the consideration of the theory of M. Dax. The brain as a whole has hitherto been considered as a symmetrical organ, even by those who regarded it as an assemblage of lesser organs arranged in pairs with corresponding functions; M. Dax, however, assigns a function to the left hemisphere, which, according to him, is not shared by the right, for he places the lesion in aphasia solely in the left hemisphere, without however limiting it to any part of that hemisphere.*

This is a question that can only be settled by a careful statistical research. M. Broca estimates the proportion of aphasics with lesion in the right hemisphere as 1 in 20. In 1864, M. Vulpian tabulated all the cases bearing upon this question which came under his observation at the La Salpêtrière. They were twelve in number, and divided as follows:—Lesions of the left anterior lobe with aphasia, 5; lesions of the left anterior lobe without aphasia, 4; lesions of the right anterior lobe without aphasia, 1; cases of aphasia without lesion of either anterior lobe, 2. Amongst the 63 cases I have recorded in the first three parts of this essay, in 32 only there was hemiplegia, the paralysis occurring 21 times on the right side and 7 times on the left, whilst in 4 instances the side was not stated. It will be remembered that M. Dax's paper contained 140 obser-

* Dr. Dax's conclusions were embodied in a communication to the medical congress held at Montpellier in the year 1836, the title of his paper being—Lésions de la moitié gauche de l'encéphale coincidant avec l'oubli des signes de la pensée. In 1863 his son, Dr. G. Dax, presented a memoir to the Academy of Medicine of Paris, in which, whilst supporting the views of his father as to the seat of speech in the left hemisphere, he confined it to more narrow limits, namely, the anterior and external part of the middle lobe.

vations confirmatory of his view. Notwithstanding numerous and well authenticated exceptions, it must be conceded that in a vast majority of instances, loss of speech occurs in conjunction with right hemiplegia, a coincidence which may perhaps be explained on physiological grounds, as we shall see presently.

Dr. Dax's theory receives valuable support from such cases as that I have quoted as occurring in the Middlesex Hospital under Dr. Stewart, where the patient retained the power of speech after an attack of left hemiplegia, but became aphasic a few days later, on the occurrence of dextral paralysis. An analogous case has recently been published by M. Auguste Voisin, the leading features of which deserve a passing allusion, not only from its clinical importance, but from the scrupulous care with which the autopsy is described.

A female, aged 55, was under the care of M. Voisin, at La Salpêtrière, for left hemiplegia of four years' duration ; speech, as well as the intellectual powers, being unimpaired. One day she was suddenly seized with giddiness, followed by complete aphasia ; at the expiration of four days, the report states that there was no recovery of speech, but that the patient made herself understood by gesture. On the fifth day death ensued. Autopsy—The membranes are normal in appearance, and are easily removed without injury to the grey substance beneath. A large number of vessels contain calcareous plates. In the right hemisphere, the 1st, 2nd, and 3rd frontal convolutions are perfectly healthy, as also the island of Reil; on opening the lateral ventricle from above, a pulpy softening is noticed of a pale yellow colour occupying the corpus striatum, without, however, involving its extra-ventricular nucleus, or extending to the grey and white substance adjoining the insula. In the left hemisphere, the 1st, 2nd, and 3rd frontal convolutions present no alteration, but not so the island of Reil, in which there is a very superficial and circumscribed softening (de 8 ou 10 millimètres de diamètre), limited to the grey matter, the subjacent white matter, as well as the extra-ventricular nucleus of the left corpus striatum, being perfectly free from disease of any kind. The neighbouring vessels are more or less infiltrated with calcareous salts, and an artery of medium calibre, destined for the nutrition of the island of Reil, is entirely obstructed by a calcareous deposit. Several portions having been submitted to microscopic examination, the following appearances were observed :—1° a large number of corpuscles of Gluge of a reddish yellow colour; 2° some crystals of hematoidine disseminated here and there, also of a decidedly reddish yellow colour; 3° a considerable number of oil globules; 4° very irregular nerve-tubes; 5° blood vessels completely discoloured, and presenting some isolated colourless corpuscles.*

M. Voisin calls attention to the fact that the interest of the above case consists in the limitation of the lesion to the grey matter of the left island of Reil, also to the complete aphasia occurring in a woman, who, for four years, had been hemiplegic on the left side from softening of the right corpus striatum; he also observes that if his attention had not been called to the loss of speech, such a circumscribed lesion might well have escaped his notice, in which case this necropsy would have swelled the number of those where no anatomical lesion could be found to explain the aphasia.

Thus the arguments in favour of M. Dax may be said to be of a positive and of a negative kind, and could we stop here, M. Dax's position might be said to be impregnable; but—audi alteram partem—there is another side to the picture, and the partisans of M. Dax must explain away certain exceptional cases, which it seems difficult to reconcile with the truth of his views.

Several cases have been recorded in which serious disorganisation of the left anterior lobe coincided with perfect integrity of speech. I have already quoted such

* Gazette des Hôpitaux, Jan. 25, 1868.

cases, and I can make but a cursory allusion to some
others that have been brought under my notice. M.
Maximin Legrand has related the history of a man who
was shot in the head during the Revolution of 1848,
and whose speech was not in the least affected, although
after death it was found that the left anterior lobe had
been shattered by the discharge from the gun.* M.
Béclard has published the case of a syphilitic patient
whose speech remained unaffected to the last, although
it was found that all the left hemisphere was reduced
to a pulp.† One of the most uncompromising opponents
of M. Dax's views is M. Lelut, whose report on M.
Dax's paper gave rise to the prolonged discussion on
this subject at the Academy of Medicine of Paris.
After inveighing in general terms against all cerebral
localisation, M. Lelut reminds the academy of a case
he had published thirty years ago, of an epileptic who
retained his speech in its integrity to the last moment,
although his entire left hemisphere was completely dis-
organised.‡

* Dictionnaire Encyclopédique des Sciences Médicales, Article
"Aphasie," par Jules Falret, p. 628.

† *Ibid*, p. 628.

‡ I give the leading features of this case in M. Lelut's own words.
It affords another illustration of the manner in which cases are distorted to suit particular theories, for on referring to the original
description as it appeared in the Journal Hebdomadaire de Médecine,
it seems that instead of complete disorganisation of the left hemisphere,
the lesion was limited to the posterior and middle lobes, and the report goes on to say that "the anterior lobes were very well developed
and their convolutions had the usual proportions." In reference to
the question we are now considering this is, doubtless, not the only
instance in which a clinical observation has been misinterpreted
according to the fancy of individual critics. M. Lelut has chosen to
cite it as militating against Dax's theory; surely Bouillaud and Broca
have a better right to claim it as pre-eminently tending to support
their views.

There is also another class of observations which seem to me to be irreconcileable with the exclusiveness of M. Dax's unilateral theory, for there exists a certain number of carefully recorded cases, in which aphasia was one of the symptoms, although the lesion was limited to the right hemisphere. I have already cited cases of this kind in our first part, and quite recently Dr. Spender, of Bath, has published an interesting case of idiopathic abscess in the *right* hemisphere, in which during life the symptoms were epileptic convulsions in the left arm and leg, and subsequently loss of speech and left hemiplegia.

I could multiply observations of a similar character to those I have mentioned, the study of which would tend to discredit the idea of locating the faculty of speech in one side of the brain to the exclusion of the other, but enough has been said to prove two things :—

1°. That aphasia certainly is not invariably connected with lesion of the left anterior lobe of the brain.

2°. That the converse of this is not true also— namely, that when a positive lesion of the left anterior lobe exists, aphasia is necessarily one of the symptoms.

I now arrive at the consideration of the views of M. Broca, whose researches lead him to confine the seat of speech to a very narrow limit—the posterior part of the third frontal convolution of the left hemisphere !

However startling this assertion may be, a considerable number of observations have been recorded, which, at first sight, would seem to substantiate it, and in the previous pages I have quoted several cases published by such careful observers as Dr. Sanders, Dr. Scoresby Jackson, and Dr. Bastian, which give a general support to this exclusive doctrine.* To my mind, however— and I say it with the greatest possible respect for the distinguished surgeon of La Pitié—of all the different theories that have been advanced, this least of all will stand the test of an impartial scrutiny.

Since the publication of M. Broca's pamphlets, the attention of the profession in all parts of the world has been directed to the question of the cerebral localisation of speech, and evidence is daily accumulating of such a nature as to undermine M. Broca's position at every point, I have already quoted cases observed by MM. Charcot, Vulpian, and Trousseau, in which aphasia existed with complete integrity of the third left frontal convolution, and it would be tedious to dwell further on this kind of evidence. It has been stated by M. Broca, and repeated by M. Jules Falret and Dr. Wm. Ogle, that there is no example of the opposite condition— namely, positive lesion of the third left frontal convolution without aphasia; it will, however, be remembered that I have quoted such a case in our second part, as reported by Dr. Simpson of the Gloucester Asylum.† Therefore, we can have aphasia without disease of the third left frontal convolution, and *vice versâ*. Further- more, M. Moreau (de Tours) has observed at La Salpêtrière a case of *congenital absence of the third left frontal convolution*, as well as of the inferior parietal and

---

* Since the above was written, M. Charcot has informed me that he has met with two cases of aphasia without hemiplegia, in which the only lesion found after death was obstruction from atheromatous de- generation of the branch of the middle cerebral artery which supplies the third left frontal convolution.

† Dr. Long Fox, of Bristol, has observed a case of syphilitic disease of the left frontal convolutions involving Broca's region, the power of speech being unimpaired. Lond. Hosp. Reports, vol. iv., p. 350.

the superior temporo-sphenoidal convolutions on the same side—or, in other words, all that part of the left hemisphere which bounds the fissure of Sylvius, and which is known in M. Foville's nomenclature as la circonvolution d'enceinte de la fissure de Sylvius, had never become developed.   Now, if the third left frontal convolution, or even its immediate neighbourhood, were the exclusive seat of speech, this patient ought to have been aphasic, which, it is stated, was not the case.*

Let us now weigh in the balance of impartial criticism the case which has served as the foundation stone upon which M. Broca has erected his theory.   I allude, of course, to the case of Tan, the details of which I have already given.   This observation has been quoted by writers in all parts of the world as a case of aphasia from lesion of the third left frontal convolution; indeed, it was the very case which resulted in the conversion of its author to the unilateral theory.   Now, on referring to the description I have given of Tan's autopsy, it will be seen that in addition to the disease in the second and third left frontal convolutions, upon which M. Broca lays such stress, the following morbid conditions were also observed;—Thickening of the cranium and of the dura mater, universal infiltration of the pia mater with yellowish plastic matter of the colour of pus.   The greater part of the left frontal lobe was softened, and a cavity of the size of a hen's egg was caused by the

* M. Broca, in commenting on this case, the importance and signifi-cance of which he fully admits, says, that when the third left frontal convolution—the ordinary seat of articulate language—is congenitally deficient, the individual learns to speak with the third right frontal convolution, just in the same way as a child born without the right hand becomes as skilful with the left, as others are with the right hand.

destruction of the inferior marginal convolution of the temporo-sphenoidal lobe, the convolutions of the island of Reil, and the subjacent part or extra-ventricular nucleus of the corpus striatum. It will also be observed that the weight of the encephalon was less by 14 ounces than the average weight of the brain in men of fifty years of age. As the softening, instead of being limited to Broca's region, involved the greater part of the left frontal lobe, surely it implies a breach of the laws of probability, to assume that the disease commenced in the third frontal convolution 21 *years before his death*, simply because the softening was most apparent at that spot which M. Broca considers was the primary seat of mischief at the period of the clinical history during which the faculty of speech alone was abolished.

I have also formed an opinion of the value of M. Broca's theory from a consideration of cases observed by myself. Of the cases that have fallen under my own observation, a careful autopsy was made in five instances, when the frontal convolutions, being examined with great care, were invariably found healthy. The clinical history of these cases is given in the third part of this essay,* but the post mortem appearances are added in four instances only, as the subject of one of them, William Sainty, was still living at the time I wrote. I will here add that he soon afterwards died from exhaustion after another epileptiform seizure, when the following appearances were noticed after death :— Cranium somewhat thickened ; dura mater much more so. Intense congestion of the convex surface of hemispheres, decidedly more marked on the left side ; considerable opacity of the arachnoid, also more marked on

* *Vide* pp. 65, 73, 76, 77, 87.

the left side. A little flattening of convex surface of
left anterior lobe. In the middle of the left posterior
lobe was a softening of about the size of an apricot; a
similar condition existed at the same spot in the right
hemisphere, but the softening was not so far advanced.
The frontal convolutions were especially examined, but
no trace of softening or other disease was discovered;
the central ganglia, pons, and cerebellum were also
healthy. There was a want of firmness in the brain
generally, but no appearance of hemispheric disease
elsewhere than as above stated, although various portions were submitted to a careful microscopic examination. All the arteries of the base of the brain were
atheromatous; the left middle cerebral was completely
filled by a fibrinous plug, and the left vertebral contained a small thin red filiform fibrinous cast, occupying
only about a quarter of the diameter of the vessel.
The heart weighed 11½ ounces; the left ventricle was
hypertrophied. Narrowing of mitral orifice with considerable atheroma at the base of the valve, as also at
the base of one of the aortic valves. Considerable
dilatation of tricuspid orifice with slight thickening of
the valve itself. The weight of the encephalon, stripped
of dura mater, was 47 ounces.

The advocates of M. Broca's views will charitably
say that there may have been some slight disease of the
frontal convolutions not patent to my means of investigation. This is an objection that may be raised against
all negative cases; but granted that there may have
been some slight change in the texture of the third left
frontal convolution not appreciable to my senses, the
whole history of this case points to the certain conclusion, that the *fons et origo mali* was in the posterior

lobes, and here must have been the commencement of disease, when, four years before his death, the first and only morbid symptom showed itself in the total suspension of the faculty of articulate language.

It will be observed that I have hitherto considered this question solely from a pathological stand-point; but it seems to me that the anatomist, the physiologist, the comparative anatomist, and the anthropologist, can do us good service, and that it is to their researches, perhaps even more than to those of the clinical physician, that we are to look for the removal of the cloud which now envelops the obscure subject of the localisation of the faculty of speech.

ANATOMY.—Let us first consider whether the study of the minute anatomy of the brain, and especially of the cerebral convolutions, can help the question of localisation. We may fairly assume that difference of structure implies difference in function, it is important, therefore, to ascertain whether the generally assumed symmetry of the two hemispheres is correct. There cannot be a doubt that in general form the two opposite sides of the brain are alike, or at all events, resemble each other so closely, that no essential difference can be appreciated by the naked eye. Dr. Todd, however, says that although the convolutions of opposite hemispheres in the human subject cannot be said to be absolutely unsymmetrical, yet a careful examination will shew that if the same convolutions exist on each side, they are of apparently different sizes, and not closely corresponding as regards situation; on the other hand, he says, that in the imperfectly developed brains of the idiot or young child, as well as of the inferior animals, the convolutions are quite symmetrical.*† M. Broca, who never takes anything for granted, and whose indefatigable zeal led him to examine forty brains, came to the conclusion that the convolutions are notably more numerous in the left frontal lobe than in the right, and that the converse condition exists in the occipital lobes, where the right is richer in convolutions than the left.

The comparative weight of the two hemispheres is an interesting point to note. The researches of M. Broca, made at Bicêtre and at La Salpêtrière, have shewn that although the difference of weight between the right and left hemispheres is scarcely appreciable,‡ yet the left frontal lobe is perceptibly heavier than the right; there would seem, therefore, to be a sort of compensation between the weights of the two frontal and the two occipital lobes, as we have already seen that the right occipital lobe is richer in convolutions and therefore presumably heavier than the left.

The question of the identity of minute structure in the different cerebral convolutions must now engage our attention. M. Baillarger distinguishes six different layers of nervous substance in the convolutions, and

* Cyclopedia of Anatomy and Physiology, vol. iii., p. 696.

† Dr. Moxon considers that education is unilateral, that the brain becomes unsymmetrical in higher and more intelligent animals, and reaches its greatest want of symmetry in man, whose early life is spent in the acquirement of what he affirms to be one-sided educational developments.—British and Foreign Medico-Chirurgical Review, vol. 37, p. 489.

‡ According to Dr. Boyd's statistics, which are based on nearly 800 cases observed at the Marylebone Infirmary, the weight of the left hemisphere almost invariably exceeded that of the right by at least the eighth of an ounce.—Philosophical Transactions, 1861, vol. 151, p. 241.

M

Dr. Lockhart Clarke says that in most of them at least seven distinct and concentric layers may be distinguished. Dr. Clarke says that the other convolutions differ from those at the extremities of the posterior lobes, not only by the comparative faintness of their several layers, but also by the appearance of some of their cells; he also adds that at the extremity of these posterior lobes the cells of all the layers are small, but on proceeding forward from this point, the convolutions are found to contain a number of cells of a much larger kind; again, in the insula which overlies the extra-ventricular portion of the corpus striatum, he finds a great number of the cells are somewhat larger, and the general aspect of the tissue is rather different. M. Broca has also studied the minute structure of the cerebral convolutions, and has ascertained that the relative thickness and general disposition of the six layers recognised by M. Baillarger differ notably in the divers regions, and although his researches are not definitely terminated, he ventures to assert that the structure of the convolutions of the insula differs from that of the frontal convolutions and of the hippocampus major. I can nowhere find that any difference has been noticed in the convolutions of the two hemispheres.*

* Since the above was written, Dr. Broadbent has kindly favoured me with a private communication in reference to his recent researches as to the course of the fibres of the brain, so far as his observations bear upon our subject. Dr. Broadbent's dissections shew that the structure of the third frontal convolution is peculiar, inasmuch as it receives fibres from a greater variety of sources than any other convolution; and he adds that although this anatomical fact does not throw any particular light on the function of the third frontal convolution, it seems to indicate that it is an important part of the hemisphere. In comparing the two sides of the brain, Dr. Broadbent has

PHYSIOLOGY.—What does physiology say to Dax's theory, which has in its favour the undoubted frequency of aphasia with right hemiplegia, as compared with loss of speech as an accompaniment of sinistral paralysis ? This may possibly be explained by the anatomical difference between the origin of the right and left carotids, making the supply of blood to the left side of the brain more direct than that to the opposite hemisphere, and by increasing its functional activity, thus rendering the left hemisphere more adapted for the exercise of speech.

It would be interesting to know what effect would be produced upon speech by cutting off the direct supply of blood from the left hemisphere. Dr. Wm. Ogle quotes a case where the left common carotid artery was tied by Mr. Lee ; the patient died in two days, and in the interval between the operation and his death he was speechless.* In the Medico-Chirurgical Transactions for 1859 and 1865, are recorded four cases in which the left common carotid was tied by Mr. Nunneley of Leeds ; speech was unaffected in three instances, but in the fourth, great difficulty in speaking was noticed on the sixth day. Since the publication of those cases Mr. Nunneley has tied the common carotid in two other instances, and he writes to say "in neither of these was there any difficulty in speech, either as regards the idea or the power of utterance."†

usually found the third frontal convolution larger on the left side than on the right, and in the brain of a deaf and dumb woman, he noted that this gyrus was small on both sides, and especially on the left.

* St. George's Hospital Reports, 1867, p. 111.

† On looking over the published cases of ligature of the common carotid artery, I find that one of the earliest instances is one where the

An important question for inquiry is, the frequency of the coincidence of left hemiplegia with aphasia in left-handed people. I can only find two instances of this combination; one recorded by Dr. Hughlings Jackson,* and the other by Dr. Wadham. The subject of Dr. Wadham's case, a young man of 18, belonged to a left-handed family, as four of his brothers, as well as himself, were left-handed. This case having terminated fatally, there was found to be an almost entire absence of the island of Reil on the right side, its place being occupied by a large cavity containing a little fluid and a small amount of broken-down brain-matter; the left hemisphere was perfectly healthy.†

As a cognate question, I would ask, why are we right-handed? Is the human race right-handed by mere accident? Although there are a few left-handed people in the world, the immense majority of persons use the right hand for every mechanical act. Is this a question of education or of mere imitation? If we concede this, we must admit that our ancestors in remote ages must have been influenced by some cause connected with the organization itself; if it were a mere chance that had determined the choice of the right hand, we should find some left-handed races in certain parts of the world, which, I believe I am right in stating, is not

left common carotid was tied in 1815, by Mr. Dalrymple, the well known Surgeon of the Norfolk and Norwich Hospital, for aneurism by anastomosis of the left orbit. It this case speech seems not to have been affected, for it is stated that "a few minutes after the patient was placed in bed, she declared that her head no longer felt like her old head, as the noise by which she had been so long tormented had now ceased."—Medico-Chirurgical Transactions, 1815, v. 6.

* Medical Times, Aug. 25, 1866.

† St. George's Hospital Reports, 1869, p. 245.

the case. Besides, this question may be set at rest, says M. Broca, by the consideration "that notwithstanding all their efforts to counteract it, there are left-handed people, who remain left-handed, and one must, in their case, admit the existence of an inverse organic predisposition, against which imitation, and even education, cannot prevail."*

The study of Embryology may assist us here. An eminent foreign physiologist, Gratiolet, says that in the development of the brain, the frontal convolutions of the left hemisphere are in advance of those of the right, and that the left are already properly figured, whilst the right are not yet even visible. Thus according to Gratiolet the left hemisphere, which holds in its dependence the movements of the right limbs, is more precocious in its development than the opposite hemisphere, and thus the young child uses by preference the limbs of which the innervation is the most complete, or in other words he becomes right-handed. From the cause which thus makes us use the left hemisphere for mechanical acts, may arise the circumstance of our using it in perference for speech, and we thus become left-brained—*gauchers du cerveau*—to use M. Broca's expression. But is this theory of the early development of the left frontal convolutions true? Gratiolet says it is; Carl Vogt, an equal authority, denies it. This is an extremely interesting and important question, about which very few are in a position to give a valid

* At the discussion on aphasia which took place at the Norwich meeting of the British Association, Professor Broca alluded to the circumstance that all birds perched on the right leg; Dr. Crisp, on the other hand, said that this peculiarity was confined to Grallæ, and he believed it was a question of equilibrium, and that the bird was compelled to take this position from the greater weight of the liver.

opinion, and I regret I can quote no British authority in reference to it.

COMPARATIVE ANATOMY.—Does the study of Comparative Anatomy throw any light upon our subject? Here we must inquire whether language be the exclusive prerogative of man? Some would answer this question in the negative, and M. Lemoine, in the work to which I have already alluded, devotes a chapter to *Le Langage des Bêtes.** The remarkable faculty of imitation and of gesticulation possessed by the Ape tribe, together with their power of giving expression to a variety of emotions, would seem to imply the possession of a faculty, to which one might properly give the name of language. Leconte, in his "History of China," says of an Ape which he saw in the Straits of Molucca, that its actions so strongly resembled those of Man, and its passions were so lively and significant, that a dumb person could scarcely make himself better understood, or more plainly express his ideas and desires.

Max Müller, speaking of this subject, says, "Speech is a specific faculty of man. It distinguishes him from all other creatures; and if we wish to acquire more definite ideas as to the real nature of human speech, all we can do is to compare man with those animals that seem to come nearest to him, and thus try to discover what he shares in common with these animals, and what is peculiar to him, and to him alone."

* A distinguished French anthropologist, M. Coudereau, says that articulate language in man is neither an innate nor an exclusive faculty; that man acquires the faculty of speech by his memory, labour, and imitation—the parrot does no more; that from a linguistic stand-point, this faculty is in its nature identical in man and animal.

Further on he says, "Language is something more palpable than a fold of the brain or an angle of the skull; it is the one great barrier between the brute and man; it admits of no cavilling, and no process of natural selection will ever distil significant words out of the notes of birds or the cries of beasts. Language is our Rubicon and no brute will dare to pass it." Without entering into the question of whether the means of communicating with each other undoubtedly possessed by brutes be entitled to the appellation of a language or not, it cannot be denied that one of the great distinctions between man and animals is the possession of articulate language. One of the differences between man and the more intelligent animals is in the degree of development of the cerebral convolutions, which, moreover, exist only in the class Mammalia; and according to Flourens, the Rodentia, the least intelligent of the Mammalia, have no convolutions; the Ruminantia, more intelligent than the Rodentia, have convolutions; the Pachydermata, who are still more intelligent than the Ruminantia, possess still more convolutions, and so on the number continues to increase as we ascend to the Carnivora, then to the Apes, the Orangs, and lastly to Man, who is the richest of all animals in cerebral convolutions. If this gradation in the number of the convolutions has a relation to the intelligence of the animals, it would seem to give an *a priori* reason for concluding that the highest product of intelligence—speech—may well have some connection with the development of the convolutional grey matter.

Let us consider for one moment the comparison which Carl Vogt makes between our quadrumanous cousins and ourselves. According to this distinguished natural-

ist, the Apes have an extremely imperfect development
of the third frontal convolution, and the same condition
exists in the Microcephali; therefore, he says, as neither
Apes nor Microcephali can speak, Comparative Anatomy
gives a subsidiary support to the theory which places
speech in this convolution. Professor Vogt's views
seem to me of such great importance, and so extremely
pertinent to our subject, that I shall give them in his
own words.

The brain of Man and that of Apes, especially of the anthro-
poid apes (Orang, Chimpanzee, Gorilla), are constructed absolutely upon the same type—a type by itself—and which is
characterised, amongst other things, by the fissure of Sylvius
and by the manner in which the island of Reil is formed and
covered; but there are secondary differences in the arrangement
of the folds, in the comparative development of the lobes and
of the convolutions. One of the principal characters is, that in
the brain of all the human races, without exception, the frontal
lobe, by its posterior and inferior part (that is in Broca's
region) touches the temporo-sphenoidal lobe, so as to give the
fissure of Sylvius with its two branches, the appearance of a
double-pronged fork; whilst in the Apes, Broca's convolution
is separated from the temporo-sphenoidal lobe by the lower end
of the transverse frontal and transverse parietal convolutions;
in other words, in Man, the third frontal convolution is extra-
ordinarily developed and covers partly the insula, whilst the
transverse central convolutions are of much less importance; in
the Ape, on the other hand, the third frontal convolution is but
slightly developed, whilst the central transverse convolutions
are very large, descending quite to the edge of the hemisphere,
and giving to the fissure of Sylvius the form of a V. The
cause of this difference dates from the period of embryonic
development:—the brain of the fœtus of any of the Mammalia
at a certain age (two months in Man), has the form of a bean
with a large infero-lateral sinus corresponding to the insula
and the surrounding parts. From the third to the fifth month,
this large space becomes covered in Man by the *very rapid*
growth of the third frontal convolution, and by the *slow* growth
of the transverse central convolutions; whilst in the Ape, it is

just the reverse, the space is filled by the *rapid* growth of the transverse central convolutions, and by the *slow* growth of the third frontal convolution. To shew the bearing all this has upon the seat of speech, I would refer to the Microcephali who do not speak—they learn to repeat certain words like parrots, but they have no articulate language. Now, the Microcephali have the same conformation of the third frontal convolution and of the central folds as Apes—they are Apes as far as the anterior portion of their brain is concerned, and especially as far as regards the environs of the fissure of Sylvius. Thus, Man speaks; Apes and Microcephali do not speak; certain observations have been recorded which seem to place language in the part which is developed in man and contracted in the Microcephali and the Ape; comparative anatomy, therefore, comes in aid of M. Broca's doctrine.*

I have reason to believe that these views of Professor Vogt are not very generally known in this country, and I need hardly allude to the extremely important bearing they have upon the question at issue. With the view of obtaining some confirmation of the statement of the arrest of development in the third frontal convolution of the microcephali, I have consulted Mr. Marshall's extremely interesting paper in the Philosophical Transactions for the year 1864, in which he gives a detailed description of the frontal convolutions of a microcephalic woman and boy, neither of whom possessed the power of articulation. In both these brains the frontal convolutions are described as being singularly short and defective as compared with their wonderfully tortuous and complex character in the perfect brain; in fact,

---

* The above is an extract from an autograph letter with which Professor Vogt has favoured me. In this communication he expresses a doubt whether we shall ever be able satisfactorily to assign "the divers functions" which compose language, to special parts of the brain, until we have a physiological analysis of articulate language, similar to that which Helmholtz has given of sight and hearing.

Mr. Marshall adds that they were far more simple than in the orang's or the chimpanzee's brain. In only one of these microcephalic brains, however, was the want of development most apparent in the third frontal convolution. Further investigations would, therefore, seem necessary before admitting with Carl Vogt that the conformation of the microcephalic brain gives a direct support to the localisation of speech in the third left frontal convolution.

As far back as 1827, M. Bouillaud instituted a series of experiments upon animals, with the view of determining the functions of the brain, and on several occasions he removed different portions of the cerebral lobes, without impairing sight or hearing; he also removed the entire hemispheres from a chicken, in whom the power of expressing pain by its peculiar cry was retained.* On one occasion he pierced with a gimlet the anterior part of the brain of a dog, from side to side, at a spot corresponding to the union of the anterior with the middle lobes—that is in the immediate neighbourhood of Broca's region. The dog survived the mutilation, but was much less intelligent than before the operation, and although he could utter cries of pain, he had entirely lost the power of barking.† As far as the present inquiry is concerned, I am aware that but little importance can be attached to these experiments, for there is little or no analogy between the cry of a chicken or the bark of a dog, and the articulate speech of a man; still, experiments of this kind may have an

* Recherches expérimentales sur les fonctions du cerveau. Journal de Physiologie, tom. x., p. 49.

† Ibid, p. 85.

indirect bearing upon our subject, and it would be extremely interesting to know what would be the effect of traumatic injury to certain regions of the anterior lobes upon the quasi-articulatory powers of the parrot.

I think that much valuable information in reference to the seat of speech may be elicited from a more careful study of the affinities and differences between the brain of man and that of animals; but this study, surely, should not be confined to the convex surface, or even to the anterior half of the hemisphere. Professor Rolleston, in a most interesting paper, has called attention to other points of difference between the brain of man and that of apes, and he attaches a great physiological value to the presence or absence of the "*bridging convolutions*," which more or less fill up the space known as the external perpendicular fissure, which separates the occipital from the parietal lobe.*

Professor Owen mentions the superior development of the hippocampus minor, as a point of distinction between man and the lower animals. According to him, in the inferior mammalia the posterior cornu of the lateral ventricle is capacious and simple, whereas in the chimpanzee and gorilla the growing walls begin to be reduced by the encroachment of a protuberance, which in the archencephala is developed into the hippocampus minor.† It will be remembered that it was in this

---

* Medical Times, Feb. 22nd and March 15th, 1862. There are many other points in Dr. Rolleston's paper, which, although having no direct bearing upon speech, afford a collateral aid to that subject, and it is impossible to overrate the value of the talented Oxford Professor's researches in this direction.

† Comparative Anatomy and Physiology of the Vertebrates, vol. iii., p 138.

lesser hippocampus that Dr. Barlow formerly located the faculty of speech.

ANTHROPOLOGY. The comparative facility of speech in different races of mankind is an interesting point to notice, and it is much to be regretted that we possess so little authentic information upon the subject.

Gratiolet has established three principal divisions of our species under the names of Frontal or Caucasian, Parietal, and Occipital or Ethiopic. He has shown that in the Caucasian the anterior fontanelle is the last to ossify, in order to permit of the greatest possible development to the frontal lobes; and that in the Ethiopic race the converse condition exists, the posterior fontanelle being the last to ossify. According to this arrangement, in the superior races the frontal lobes of the hemispheres continue to develop themselves for a long time after the occlusion of the posterior sutures has put an end to the growth of the rest of the brain; in the inferior races, on the contrary, the ossification of the sutures proceeds from before backwards, and thus the anterior parts of the brain are first arrested in their growth.

Of course, the above arrangement only tends to prove that the development of the higher faculties of the intellect is in relation with the development of the anterior region of the skull;* it has, however, an in-

---

* With the view of verifying the accuracy of this statement, M. Broca examined the heads of thirty-two house-surgeons who had successively resided at Bicêtre during the years 1861—1862, and compared their dimensions with those of the heads of twenty-four porters attached to the various wards of the same hospital. This comparison resulted in the confirmation of the generally received opinion, that the anterior lobes are the seat of the highest order of intellectual faculties.

direct connection with the power of speech—the greatest of all men's mental attributes.

If it be true that simplicity in the arrangement of the convolutions of the brain is a mark of structural inferiority, and that a want of symmetry between the convolutions of the two hemispheres is one of the signs of intellectual superiority,* it would be extremely interesting to notice the relation between these two characters and the degree of facility of speech in the different races of mankind.

Having now considered the subject of speech, its loss, and its localisation, in all its various phases and aspects, I would observe that I am aware that my remarks may be said to be of an iconoclastic character. I may be told that I have set up the authors of the four popular theories for the mere pleasure of knocking them down again, without substituting any theory of my own in their place.

In reference to these doctrines, the truth and value of which I have called in question, it is no fault of mine if the pedestals upon which they stand are rotten. In lieu of offering any hypothesis myself as to where the cerebral centre for speech may be, I would ask, is it certain that there is a cerebral centre for speech at all ? When we talk of the "*faculty of speech*," have we any very clear and definite notions as to what we mean ?† May not speech be one of those attributes,

* Todd—loco citato.

† Dr. Maudsley denies the existence of a speech faculty, and says, "There is no more a special faculty of speech in the mind than there is a special faculty of dancing, or of writing, or of gesticulating."

the comprehension of which is beyond the limits of our finite minds? Does the loss of it necessarily imply organic lesion of structure? If it were so, how can we account for the instances I have quoted, in which the restoration of the power of speech was due to the effect of a severe mental shock?* The brilliant experiments of Dr. Richardson, of freezing the cerebrum of animals —which it has been my privilege to witness—conclusively show that various cerebral functions may be temporarily, but completely, suspended, without leaving any trace of organic mischief; and I confidently predict that the question of the localisation of our different faculties is destined to receive considerable elucidation from Dr. Richardson's valuable researches.

It has occurred to me to inquire whether during the anæsthesia produced by the inhalation of chloroform, there is any altered structural state of the cerebral tissue, which would be patent to our senses, supposing we were in a condition to make the necessary examination. From experiments lately made in Paris by Dr. Ferraud, it would seem that the action of chloroform on the cerebral nerve tissue is direct by means of the olfactory nerves, and that the production of the anæsthetic condition does not necessitate the passage of the drug into the arterial system by means of the pulmonary mucous membrane.*

---

* *Vide* Part V., pp. 138, 139.

* I am aware that the above conclusions are disputed by other physiologists (MM. Dieulafoy and Krishaber). M. Ferraud's experiments, however, seem to me to be conclusive; having opened the trachea in rabbits, he introduced a tube, and then divided the trachea above; a small cupping glass, containing a sponge imbibed with chloroform, was then placed over the nose of the rabbit; in three

May not loss or lesion of speech depend on some altered state of the cerebral tissue not appreciable to the sense of vision—to the eye—for microscopic examination is only the aided eye? Without doubt, there may be changes going on in nerve tissue which escape our means of investigation, and I am supported in this view by one of the greatest continental histologists, who, in conversing with me about softening of the brain, said that he believed there were changes of structure not revealed by the microscope, but which were patent to the sense of touch. I find that Dr. Sankey is of the same opinion, for he thinks the altered specific gravity of the brain in old people indicates that the nerve tissue has undergone some change of structure which the microscope has not yet made palpable to our vision.*

The fact of the occasional benefit obtained from the use of electricity in impaired speech, as observed by Dr. Marcet and others, would lead to the inference that the defect may depend in some instances upon an altered electrical condition. "It may be," says Dr. Beale, "that each little brain cell, with its connected fibres, in some way resembles a minute voltaic battery with its wires; the matter of which the cell is composed undergoing chemical change, in the course of which

minutes the anæsthetic condition was produced, and maintained as long as the olfactory apparatus was submitted to the action of chloroform. When the same animal was chloroformed by means of the tracheal tube and the respiratory apparatus, anæsthesia was produced a little sooner (*i.e.*, by 15 seconds) than when the anæsthetic was administered by the olfactory apparatus. Gazette des Hôpitaux, May 29, 1869.

* On the state of the Small Arteries and Capillaries in Mental Disease. Journ. Ment. Science, Jan., 1869.

slight electrical currents are developed; these being transmitted by the fibres ramifying to different parts, exert an influence upon tissues and organs amongst which they ramify."*

May not some thermal change, the result of chemical action, interfere with the exercise of speech? Here I would observe that although we are living in an age when organic chemistry is vastly increasing our knowledge of the essential nature of disease, writers on disorders of the nervous system have paid but little attention to the chemical pathology of the brain, although Dr. Adam Addison has paved the way for more extensive researches on this subject by his extremely interesting and highly original paper in the Journal of Mental Science for July, 1866, in which he very justly says he is treading on a field which is a *terra incognita* of unknown extent. The result of Dr. Addison's observations—which are all the more valuable because they are controlled by comparison with those of Bibra, L'Héritier, Schlossberger and others—is as follows :—

1°. That the different anatomical parts of one and the same brain present great differences in their quantities of water and fat.

2°. That the grey substance is far poorer in fat than the white.

3°. That the quantity of matters soluble in ether, stands in an inverse relation to the quantity of water.

4°. That the quantities of phosphorus do not have a parallel connexion with the degree of intelligence.

5°. That in three cases of hemiplegia the average quantity of fat in the corpus striatum, optic thalamus, and grey substance of the hemisphere opposite the paralysis, was less than the average quantity in the same parts of the other side.

* Lectures on the Germinal or Living Matter of Living Beings. Medical Times, July 10, 1869.

I trust that Dr. Addison may be induced to supplement his most useful essay by a special chemical analysis of those particular portions of the brain in which the seat of speech has been severally placed by the various authors who have written upon the subject.

Practitioners of the healing art are no longer divided, as in the good old days of yore, into solidists and humorists, and I am inclined to think that in our over anxiety to connect every disorder, in some way or other, with structural lesion, we are apt to overlook the condition of the fluids of the body, and in corroboration of this view I would refer to the recorded cases of loss of speech from the effect of certain drugs such as Stramonium, Belladonna, also from the introduction into the lymphatic system of a poison from the bite of a snake. Possibly the discovery of the perivascular canals of His, and of the existence of miliary aneurisms in the minute arteries of the brain, may serve as an element for a better understanding of certain functional disturbances of that organ.*

In bringing this long dissertation to a close, I wish to add that I am painfully sensible of the great disproportion which exists between the demands of this important subject, and the capacity of the person who has undertaken to deal with it; and my own sense of

---

* In the elaborate paper by Dr. Sankey, to which I have already referred, is the following passage corroborative of these views :—" Each act of cerebration (which results from an action of the blood and the cerebral tissue) requires that the blood be unimpaired in quality, and of a just quantity; blood impaired as to quality produces imperfect cerebration as proved by the injection of poisons into the blood, by the action of certain drugs which are known to enter the circulation."

N

inadequacy is enhanced by the consideration, that although one of the most learned scientific bodies in the
world devoted the long period of two months to its
elucidation, the discussion in the Academy of Medicine
of Paris terminated, without a solution of the difficulties
which its members had attempted to grapple with.

No subject of late years has so occupied the attention
of physiologists in all parts of the world, as the attempt
to localise the grand attribute of humanity, the faculty
of speech; but, I am bound to say that in spite of all
that has been written in reference to it, the question
must still be considered as *sub judice*, and an impartial
sifting of the mass of evidence I have accumulated has
led me to the following conclusions:—

1°—That although something may be said in favour
of each of the popular theories of the localisation of
speech, still, so many exceptions to each of them have
been recorded, that they will none of them bear the
test of a disinterested and impartial scrutiny.

2°—That I by no means consider it proved that there
is a cerebral centre for speech at all, and I would venture to suggest that speech, like the soul, may be something, the comprehension of which is beyond the limits
of our finite minds.

I have heard it said in reference to this inquiry, *cui
bono?* What good purpose is served by the numerous
and extensive researches which have been, and are still
being made to decide whether we have, or have not, a
portion of our cerebral substance, to which belongs the
exclusive prerogative of presiding over articulate language? Now to this objection I would apply the trite
remark that all knowledge is power; besides, surely no

subject is more worthy of the careful investigation of all labourers in the field of science than the origin of speech; it is one of the questions in which the physiologist and the student of language meet, and now that the sluice-gates of public opinion are opened upon it, error will be swept away, and a fresh impulse be given to the study of the mind. Moreover, the scientific result of the recent researches about the seat of speech, need not necessarily be limited to the acquisition of a better knowledge of the conditions under which that faculty is developed or lost; for since the attention of the profession has been directed to the investigation of the causes which interfere with the exercise of speech, a new flood of light has been thrown upon the minute anatomy and physiology of the nervous centres, which may eventually lead to the localisation of our other faculties.

The definite solution of the question I have been discussing has been retarded by the fact that authors, in many instances, have written with pre-conceived notions, and their works bear the impress of a desire to prove one theory as against another, rather than to place on record facts which may, as it were, speak for themselves. Some not wishing to leave the scientific rut in which they have so long moved, content themselves with boldly asserting that this or that theory cannot be—that it is contrary to common sense, and is the annihilation of all traditional scientific data. Others decline to discuss the unilateral theory, on the ground that it is impossible that a perfectly symmetrical organ like the brain should possess a property in one hemisphere not appertaining to the other. Now the question is not so much how it is, but if it is. In an inquiry of this kind we must dismiss all pre-conceived opinions and notions, and if physiological experiments well made, if rigorous pathological observations confirmed by necroscopic verification, should happen to furnish a number of facts sufficiently significant to establish an evident relation between certain functional alterations of speech, and the lesion of certain definite parts of the encephalon; in that case, all conjectural propositions, and all bold assertions, must vanish before the light of scientific truth.

It is in the spirit of the above remarks that I have endeavoured to approach this inquiry, and if in my attempt to unravel the difficulties with which this subject is surrounded, I have only succeeded in making "confusion worse confounded," I would say with Heberden—"*Fateor equidem ea esse rudia, inchoata, et manca; cujus rei culpa, ut maximam partem in me recidat, partim tamen in ipsius artis conditionem erit rejicienda.*"

The End.

JARROLD AND SONS, PRINTERS, NORWICH.

London, New Burlington Street,
April, 1870.

MESSRS. CHURCHILL & SONS'

Publications,

IN

MEDICINE

AND THE VARIOUS BRANCHES OF

NATURAL SCIENCE.

THE HALF-YEARLY ABSTRACT OF THE MEDICAL SCIENCES.
BEING A DIGEST OF BRITISH AND CONTINENTAL MEDICINE,
AND OF THE PROGRESS OF MEDICINE AND THE COLLATERAL SCIENCES.

Edited by W. Domett Stone, M.D., F.R.C.S., L.S.A.

Post 8vo. cloth, 6s. 6d. Vols. I. to L.

"American physicians may be congratulated that they are once more favoured with the reprint of 'Ranking's Abstract.' If any doctor is so busy that he can read but a single volume a year, then, assuredly, he should make this his book; for here are collected and condensed the most valuable contributions to periodical medical literature—French, German, British, and American—for the year; and, on the other hand, no physician—it matters not how wide the range of his reading—can fail to find, in this volume, truths that will enlarge his medical knowledge, and precepts that will help him in some of his daily professional needs."— *Cincinnati Journal of Medicine,* April, 1867.

"We have only space to say that this volume is rich in valuable articles, among which there are many on materia medica and therapeutics. Gathered from all sources in the new books and medical journals of Europe and America, this work may be viewed as the cream of that class of medical essays, and is a useful occupant of the physician's office-table, to keep him reminded of the progress of medicine."— *American Journal of Pharmacy,* May, 1867.

A CLASSIFIED INDEX

TO

MESSRS. CHURCHILL & SONS' CATALOGUE.

TO BE COMPLETED IN TWELVE PARTS, 4TO., AT 7s. 6d. PER PART.

PARTS I. & II. NOW READY.

A DESCRIPTIVE TREATISE
ON THE
NERVOUS SYSTEM OF MAN,
WITH THE MANNER OF DISSECTING IT.

By LUDOVIC HIRSCHFELD,
DOCTOR OF MEDICINE OF THE UNIVERSITIES OF PARIS AND WARSAW, PROFESSOR OF ANATOMY TO THE
FACULTY OF MEDICINE OF WARSAW;

Edited in English (from the French Edition of 1866)

By ALEXANDER MASON MACDOUGAL, F.R.C.S.,
WITH
AN ATLAS OF ARTISTICALLY-COLOURED ILLUSTRATIONS,

Embracing the Anatomy of the entire Cerebro-Spinal and Sympathetic Nervous Centres and Distributions in their accurate relations with all the important Constituent Parts of the Human Economy, and embodied in a series of 56 Single and 9 Double Plates, comprising 197 Illustrations,

Designed from Dissections prepared by the Author, and Drawn on Stone by

J. B. LÉVEILLÉ.

WILLIAM ACTON, M.R.C.S.

I.

A PRACTICAL TREATISE ON DISEASES OF THE URINARY
AND GENERATIVE ORGANS IN BOTH SEXES. Third Edition. 8vo. cloth, £1. 1s. With Plates, £1. 11s. 6d. The Plates alone, limp cloth, 10s. 6d.

II.

THE FUNCTIONS AND DISORDERS OF THE REPRODUC-
TIVE ORGANS IN CHILDHOOD, YOUTH, ADULT AGE, AND ADVANCED LIFE, considered in their Physiological, Social, and Moral Relations. Fourth Edition. 8vo. cloth, 10s. 6d.

III.

PROSTITUTION: Considered in its Moral, Social, and Sanitary Aspects,
Second Edition, enlarged. 8vo. cloth, 12s.

ROBERT ADAMS, A.M., C.M., M.D.

A TREATISE ON RHEUMATIC GOUT; OR, CHRONIC
RHEUMATIC ARTHRITIS. 8vo. cloth, with a Quarto Atlas of Plates, 21s.

WILLIAM ADAMS, F.R.C.S.

I.

ON THE PATHOLOGY AND TREATMENT OF LATERAL
AND OTHER FORMS OF CURVATURE OF THE SPINE. With Plates. 8vo. cloth, 10s. 6d.

II.

CLUBFOOT: its Causes, Pathology, and Treatment. Jacksonian Prize Essay
for 1864. With 100 Engravings. 8vo. cloth, 12s.

III.

ON THE REPARATIVE PROCESS IN HUMAN TENDONS
AFTER SUBCUTANEOUS DIVISION FOR THE CURE OF DEFORMITIES. With Plates. 8vo. cloth, 6s.

IV.

SKETCH OF THE PRINCIPLES AND PRACTICE OF
SUBCUTANEOUS SURGERY. 8vo. cloth, 2s. 6d.

WILLIAM ADDISON, F.R.C.P., F.R.S.

I.

CELL THERAPEUTICS. 8vo. cloth, 4s.

II.

ON HEALTHY AND DISEASED STRUCTURE, AND THE TRUE
PRINCIPLES OF TREATMENT FOR THE CURE OF DISEASE, ESPECIALLY CONSUMPTION AND SCROFULA, founded on MICROSCOPICAL ANALYSIS. 8vo. cloth, 12s.

C. J. B. ALDIS, M.D., F.R.C.P.

AN INTRODUCTION TO HOSPITAL PRACTICE IN VARIOUS
COMPLAINTS; with Remarks on their Pathology and Treatment. 8vo. cloth, 5s. 6d.

SOMERVILLE SCOTT ALISON, M.D.EDIN., F.R.C.P.

THE PHYSICAL EXAMINATION OF THE CHEST IN PUL-
MONARY CONSUMPTION, AND ITS INTERCURRENT DISEASES. With Engravings. 8vo. cloth, 12s.

JULIUS ALTHAUS, M.D., M.R.C.P.

ON EPILEPSY, HYSTERIA, AND ATAXY. Cr. 8vo. cloth, 4s.

THE ANATOMICAL REMEMBRANCER; OR, COMPLETE POCKET ANATOMIST. Sixth Edition, carefully Revised. 32mo. cloth, 3s. 6d.

McCALL ANDERSON, M.D., F.F.P.S.

I.

THE PARASITIC AFFECTIONS OF THE SKIN. Second Edition. With Engravings. 8vo. cloth, 7s. 6d.

II.

ECZEMA. Second Edition. 8vo. cloth, 6s.

III.

PSORIASIS AND LEPRA. With Chromo-lithograph. 8vo. cloth, 5s.

ANDREW ANDERSON, M.D.

TEN LECTURES INTRODUCTORY TO THE STUDY OF FEVER. Post 8vo. cloth, 5s.

J. T. ARLIDGE, M.D.LOND., F.R.C.P.

ON THE STATE OF LUNACY AND THE LEGAL PROVISION FOR THE INSANE; with Observations on the Construction and Organisation of Asylums. 8vo. cloth, 7s.

ALEXANDER ARMSTRONG, M.D., F.R.C.P., R.N.

OBSERVATIONS ON NAVAL HYGIENE AND SCURVY. More particularly as the latter appeared during a Polar Voyage. 8vo. cloth, 5s.

T. J. ASHTON, M.R.C.S.

I.

ON THE DISEASES, INJURIES, AND MALFORMATIONS OF THE RECTUM AND ANUS. Fourth Edition. 8vo. cloth, 8s.

II.

PROLAPSUS, FISTULA IN ANO, AND OTHER DISEASES OF THE RECTUM; their Pathology and Treatment. Third Edition. Post 8vo. cloth, 3s. 6d.

THOS. J. AUSTIN, M.R.C.S.ENG.

A PRACTICAL ACCOUNT OF GENERAL PARALYSIS: Its Mental and Physical Symptoms, Statistics, Causes, Seat, and Treatment. 8vo. cloth, 6s.

THOMAS BALLARD, M.D.

A NEW AND RATIONAL EXPLANATION OF THE DIS-EASES PECULIAR TO INFANTS AND MOTHERS; with obvious Suggestions for their Prevention and Cure. Post 8vo. cloth, 4s. 6d.

A. W. BARCLAY, M.D., F.R.C.P.

I.

A MANUAL OF MEDICAL DIAGNOSIS. Second Edition.
Foolscap 8vo. cloth, 8s. 6d.

II.

MEDICAL ERRORS.—Fallacies connected with the Application of the
Inductive Method of Reasoning to the Science of Medicine. Post 8vo. cloth, 5s.

III.

GOUT AND RHEUMATISM IN RELATION TO DISEASE
OF THE HEART. Post 8vo. cloth, 5s.

G. H. BARLOW, M.D., F.R.C.P.

A MANUAL OF THE PRACTICE OF MEDICINE. Second
Edition. Fcap. 8vo. cloth, 12s. 6d.

ROBERT BARNES, M.D., F.R.C.P.

LECTURES ON OBSTETRIC OPERATIONS, INCLUDING
THE TREATMENT OF HÆMORRHAGE, and forming a Guide to the Management of Difficult Labour. With nearly 100 Engravings. 8vo. cloth, 15s.

E. BASCOME, M.D.

A HISTORY OF EPIDEMIC PESTILENCES, FROM THE
EARLIEST AGES. 8vo. cloth, 8s.

W. R. BASHAM, M.D., F.R.C.P.

I.

RENAL DISEASES; a CLINICAL GUIDE to their DIAGNOSIS
and TREATMENT. 8vo. cloth, 7s.

II.

ON DROPSY, AND ITS CONNECTION WITH DISEASES OF
THE KIDNEYS, HEART, LUNGS AND LIVER. With 16 Plates. Third
Edition. 8vo. cloth, 12s. 6d.

H. F. BAXTER, M.R.C.S.L.

ON ORGANIC POLARITY; showing a Connexion to exist between
Organic Forces and Ordinary Polar Forces. Crown 8vo. cloth, 5s.

LIONEL J. BEALE, M.R.C.S.

THE LAWS OF HEALTH IN THEIR RELATIONS TO MIND
AND BODY. A Series of Letters from an Old Practitioner to a Patient. Post 8vo.
cloth, 7s. 6d.

LIONEL S. BEALE, M.B., F.R.S., F.R.C.P.

I.

ON KIDNEY DISEASES, URINARY DEPOSITS, AND
CALCULOUS DISORDERS. Third Edition, much Enlarged. With 70 Plates.
8vo. cloth, 25s.

II.

THE MICROSCOPE, IN ITS APPLICATION TO PRACTICAL
MEDICINE. Third Edition. With 58 Plates. 8vo. cloth, 16s.

III.

PROTOPLASM; OR, LIFE, MATTER AND MIND. Second
Edition. With 6 Plates. Crown 8vo. cloth, 6s. 6d.

HENRY BEASLEY.

I.

THE BOOK OF PRESCRIPTIONS; containing 3000 Prescriptions. Collected from the Practice of the most eminent Physicians and Surgeons, English and Foreign. Third Edition. 18mo. cloth, 6s.

II.

THE DRUGGIST'S GENERAL RECEIPT-BOOK; comprising a copious Veterinary Formulary and Table of Veterinary Materia Medica; Patent and Proprietary Medicines, Druggists' Nostrums, &c.; Perfumery, Skin Cosmetics, Hair Cosmetics, and Teeth Cosmetics; Beverages, Dietetic Articles, and Condiments; Trade Chemicals, Miscellaneous Preparations and Compounds used in the Arts, &c.; with useful Memoranda and Tables. Sixth Edition. 18mo. cloth, 6s.

III.

THE POCKET FORMULARY AND SYNOPSIS OF THE BRITISH AND FOREIGN PHARMACOPŒIAS; comprising standard and approved Formulæ for the Preparations and Compounds employed in Medical Practice. Eighth Edition, corrected and enlarged. 18mo. cloth, 6s.

HENRY BENNET, M.D.

I.

A PRACTICAL TREATISE ON UTERINE DISEASES. Fourth Edition, revised, with Additions. 8vo. cloth, 16s.

II.

WINTER AND SPRING ON THE SHORES OF THE MEDI-TERRANEAN: OR, THE RIVIERA, MENTONE, ITALY, CORSICA, SICILY, ALGERIA, SPAIN, AND BIARRITZ, AS WINTER CLIMATES. Fourth Edition, with numerous Plates, Maps, and Wood Engravings. Post 8vo. cloth, 12s.

ROBERT BENTLEY, F.L.S.

A MANUAL OF BOTANY. With nearly 1,200 Engravings on Wood. Fcap. 8vo. cloth, 12s. 6d.

ALBERT J. BERNAYS, PH.D., F.C.S.

NOTES FOR STUDENTS IN CHEMISTRY; being a Syllabus compiled from the Manuals of Miller, Fownes, Berzelius, Gerhardt, Gorup-Besanez, &c. Fifth Edition. Fcap. 8vo. cloth, 3s. 6d.

HENRY HEATHER BIGG.

ORTHOPRAXY: a complete Guide to the Modern Treatment of Deformities by Mechanical Appliances. With 300 Engravings. Second Edition. Post 8vo. cloth, 10s.

S. B. BIRCH M.D., M.R.C.P.

I.

OXYGEN: ITS ACTION, USE, AND VALUE IN THE TREATMENT OF VARIOUS DISEASES OTHERWISE INCURABLE OR VERY INTRACTABLE. Second Edition. Post 8vo. cloth, 3s. 6d.

II.

CONSTIPATED BOWELS: the Various Causes and the Different Means of Cure. Third Edition. Post 8vo. cloth, 3s. 6d.

GOLDING BIRD, M.D., F.R.S.

URINARY DEPOSITS; THEIR DIAGNOSIS, PATHOLOGY,

AND THERAPEUTICAL INDICATIONS. With Engravings. Fifth Edition.
Edited by E. LLOYD BIRKETT, M.D. Post 8vo. cloth, 10s. 6d.

JOHN BISHOP, F.R.C.S., F.R.S.

I.

ON DEFORMITIES OF THE HUMAN BODY, their Pathology

and Treatment. With Engravings on Wood. 8vo. cloth, 10s.

II.

ON ARTICULATE SOUNDS, AND ON THE CAUSES AND

CURE OF IMPEDIMENTS OF SPEECH. 8vo. cloth, 4s.

BLAINE.

OUTLINES OF THE VETERINARY ART; OR, A TREATISE

ON THE ANATOMY, PHYSIOLOGY, AND DISEASES OF THE HORSE,
NEAT CATTLE, AND SHEEP. Seventh Edition. By Charles Steel, M.R.C.V.S.L.
With Plates. 8vo. cloth, 18s.

C. L. BLOXAM.

I.

CHEMISTRY, INORGANIC AND ORGANIC; with Experiments

and a Comparison of Equivalent and Molecular Formulæ. With 276 Engravings on Wood.
8vo. cloth, 16s.

II.

LABORATORY TEACHING; OR PROGRESSIVE EXERCISES

IN PRACTICAL CHEMISTRY. With 89 Engravings. Crown, 8vo. cloth, 5s. 6d.

HONORÉ BOURGUIGNON, M.D.

ON THE CATTLE PLAGUE; OR, CONTAGIOUS TYPHUS IN

HORNED CATTLE: its History, Origin, Description, and Treatment. Post 8vo. 5s.

JOHN E. BOWMAN, & C. L. BLOXAM.

I.

PRACTICAL CHEMISTRY, including Analysis. With numerous Illus-

trations on Wood. Fifth Edition. Foolscap 8vo. cloth, 6s. 6d.

II.

MEDICAL CHEMISTRY; with Illustrations on Wood. Fourth Edition,

carefully revised. Fcap. 8vo. cloth, 6s. 6d.

P. MURRAY BRAIDWOOD, M.D. EDIN.

ON PYÆMIA, OR SUPPURATIVE FEVER: the Astley Cooper

Prize Essay for 1868. With 12 Plates. 8vo. cloth, 10s. 6d.

JAMES BRIGHT, M.D.

ON DISEASES OF THE HEART, LUNGS, & AIR PASSAGES;

with a Review of the several Climates recommended in these Affections. Third Edition. Post 8vo. cloth, 9s.

WILLIAM BRINTON, M.D., F.R.S.

I.

THE DISEASES OF THE STOMACH, with an Introduction on its
Anatomy and Physiology; being Lectures delivered at St. Thomas's Hospital. Second
Edition. 8vo. cloth, 10s. 6d.　　II.

INTESTINAL OBSTRUCTION. Edited by DR. BUZZARD. Post 8vo.
cloth, 5s.

BERNARD E. BRODHURST, F.R.C.S.

I.

CURVATURES OF THE SPINE: their Causes, Symptoms, Pathology,
and Treatment. Second Edition. Roy. 8vo. cloth, with Engravings, 7s. 6d.

II.

ON THE NATURE AND TREATMENT OF CLUBFOOT AND
ANALOGOUS DISTORTIONS involving the TIBIO-TARSAL ARTICULATION.
With Engravings on Wood. 8vo. cloth, 4s. 6d.

III.

PRACTICAL OBSERVATIONS ON THE DISEASES OF THE
JOINTS INVOLVING ANCHYLOSIS, and on the TREATMENT for the
RESTORATION of MOTION. Third Edition, much enlarged, 8vo. cloth, 4s. 6d.

CHARLES BROOKE, M.A., M.B., F.R.S.

ELEMENTS OF NATURAL PHILOSOPHY. Based on the Work of
the late Dr. Golding Bird. Sixth Edition. With 700 Engravings. Fcap. 8vo. cloth, 12s. 6d.

T. L. BRUNTON, B.Sc., M.B.

ON DIGITALIS. With some Observations on the Urine. Fcap. 8vo.
cloth, 4s. 6d.

THOMAS BRYANT, F.R.C.S.

I.

ON THE DISEASES AND INJURIES OF THE JOINTS.
CLINICAL AND PATHOLOGICAL OBSERVATIONS. Post 8vo. cloth, 7s. 6d.

II.

CLINICAL SURGERY. Parts I. to VII. 8vo., 3s. 6d. each.

FLEETWOOD BUCKLE, M.D., L.R.C.P.LOND.

VITAL AND ECONOMICAL STATISTICS OF THE HOSPITALS,
INFIRMARIES, &c., OF ENGLAND AND WALES. Royal 8vo. 5s.

JOHN CHARLES BUCKNILL, M.D., F.R.C.P., F.R.S., & DANIEL H. TUKE, M.D.

A MANUAL OF PSYCHOLOGICAL MEDICINE: containing
the History, Nosology, Description, Statistics, Diagnosis, Pathology, and Treatment of
Insanity. Second Edition. 8vo. cloth, 15s.

GEORGE BUDD, M.D., F.R.C.P., F.R.S.

I.

ON DISEASES OF THE LIVER.
Illustrated with Coloured Plates and Engravings on Wood. Third Edition. 8vo. cloth, 16s.

II.

ON THE ORGANIC DISEASES AND FUNCTIONAL DIS-
ORDERS OF THE STOMACH. 8vo. cloth, 9s.

G. W. CALLENDER, F.R.C.S.

FEMORAL RUPTURE : Anatomy of the Parts concerned. With Plates.
8vo. cloth, 4s.

JOHN M. CAMPLIN, M.D., F.L.S.

ON DIABETES, AND ITS SUCCESSFUL TREATMENT.
Third Edition, by Dr. Glover. Fcap. 8vo. cloth, 3s. 6d.

ROBERT B. CARTER, F.R.C.S.

ON THE INFLUENCE OF EDUCATION AND TRAINING
IN PREVENTING DISEASES OF THE NERVOUS SYSTEM. Fcap. 8vo., 6s.

W. B. CARPENTER, M.D., F.R.S.

I.

PRINCIPLES OF HUMAN PHYSIOLOGY. With nearly 300 Illustrations on Steel and Wood. Seventh Edition. Edited by Mr. HENRY POWER. 8vo. cloth, 28s.

II.

A MANUAL OF PHYSIOLOGY. With 252 Illustrations on Steel and Wood. Fourth Edition. Fcap. 8vo. cloth, 12s. 6d.

III.

THE MICROSCOPE AND ITS REVELATIONS. With more than 400 Engravings on Steel and Wood. Fourth Edition. Fcap. 8vo. cloth, 12s. 6d.

JOSEPH PEEL CATLOW, M.R.C.S.

ON THE PRINCIPLES OF ÆSTHETIC MEDICINE; or the
Natural Use of Sensation and Desire in the Maintenance of Health and the Treatment of Disease. 8vo. cloth, 9s.

T. K. CHAMBERS, M.D., F.R.C.P.

I.

LECTURES, CHIEFLY CLINICAL. Fourth Edition. 8vo. cloth, 14s.

II.

THE INDIGESTIONS OR DISEASES OF THE DIGESTIVE
ORGANS FUNCTIONALLY TREATED. Second Edition. 8vo. cloth, 10s. 6d.

III.

SOME OF THE EFFECTS OF THE CLIMATE OF ITALY.
Crown 8vo. cloth, 4s. 6d.

H. T. CHAPMAN, F.R.C.S.

I.

THE TREATMENT OF OBSTINATE ULCERS AND CUTA-
NEOUS ERUPTIONS OF THE LEG WITHOUT CONFINEMENT. Third Edition. Post 8vo. cloth, 3s. 6d.

II.

VARICOSE VEINS : their Nature, Consequences, and Treatment, Palliative and Curative. Second Edition. Post 8vo. cloth, 3s. 6d.

PYE HENRY CHAVASSE, F.R.C.S.

I.

ADVICE TO A MOTHER ON THE MANAGEMENT OF
HER CHILDREN. Tenth Edition. Foolscap 8vo., 2s. 6d.

II.

COUNSEL TO A MOTHER: being a Continuation and the Completion
of " Advice to a Mother." Fcap. 8vo. 2s. 6d.

III.

ADVICE TO A WIFE ON THE MANAGEMENT OF HER
OWN HEALTH. With an Introductory Chapter, especially addressed to a Young
Wife. Ninth Edition. Fcap. 8vo., 2s. 6d.

F. LE GROS CLARK, F.R.C.S.

I.

LECTURES ON THE PRINCIPLES OF SURGICAL DIAG-
NOSIS : ESPECIALLY IN RELATION TO SHOCK AND VISCERAL
LESIONS   Delivered at the Royal College of Surgeons. 8vo. cloth, 10s. 6d.

II.

OUTLINES OF SURGERY ; being an Epitome of the Lectures on the
Principles and the Practice of Surgery delivered at St. Thomas's Hospital. Fcap. 8vo.
cloth, 5s.

JOHN CLAY, M.R.C.S.

KIWISCH ON DISEASES OF THE OVARIES: Translated, by
permission, from the last German Edition of his Clinical Lectures on the Special Pathology and Treatment of the Diseases of Women. With Notes, and an Appendix on the
Operation of Ovariotomy. Royal 12mo. cloth, 16s.

JOHN COCKLE, M.D., F.R.C.P.

ON INTRA-THORACIC CANCER. 8vo. 6s. 6d.

MAURICE H. COLLIS, M.D.DUB., F.R.C.S.I.

THE DIAGNOSIS AND TREATMENT OF CANCER AND
THE TUMOURS ANALOGOUS TO IT. With coloured Plates. 8vo. cloth, 14s.

A. J. COOLEY.

THE CYCLOPÆDIA OF PRACTICAL RECEIPTS, PRO-
CESSES, AND COLLATERAL INFORMATION IN THE ARTS, MANU-
FACTURES, PROFESSIONS, AND TRADES, INCLUDING MEDICINE,
PHARMACY, AND DOMESTIC ECONOMY; designed as a General Book of
Reference for the Manufacturer, Tradesman, Amateur, and Heads of Families. Fourth
and greatly enlarged Edition, 8vo. cloth, 28s.

W. WHITE COOPER, F.R.C.S.

I.

ON WOUNDS AND INJURIES OF THE EYE. Illustrated by
17 Coloured Figures and 41 Woodcuts. * 8vo. cloth, 12s.

II.

ON NEAR SIGHT, AGED SIGHT, IMPAIRED VISION,
AND THE MEANS OF ASSISTING SIGHT. With 31 Illustrations on Wood.
Second Edition. Fcap. 8vo. cloth, 7s. 6d.

S. COOPER.

A DICTIONARY OF PRACTICAL SURGERY AND ENCYCLO-
PÆDIA OF SURGICAL SCIENCE. New Edition, brought down to the present time. By SAMUEL A. LANE, F.R.C.S., assisted by various eminent Surgeons. Vol. I., 8vo. cloth, £1. 5s.

HOLMES COOTE, F.R.C.S.

A REPORT ON SOME IMPORTANT POINTS IN THE
TREATMENT OF SYPHILIS. 8vo. cloth, 5s.

R. P. COTTON, M.D., F.R.C.P.

PHTHISIS AND THE STETHOSCOPE; OR, THE PHYSICAL
SIGNS OF CONSUMPTION. Fourth Edition. Foolscap 8vo. cloth, 3s. 6d.

WILLIAM COULSON, F.R.C.S.

ON DISEASES OF THE BLADDER AND PROSTATE GLAND.
New Edition, revised. *In Preparation.*

WALTER J. COULSON, F.R.C.S.

I.

A TREATISE ON SYPHILIS. 8vo. cloth, 10s.

II.

STONE IN THE BLADDER: Its Prevention, Early Symptoms, and
Treatment by Lithotrity. 8vo. cloth, 6s.

T. B. CURLING, F.R.C.S., F.R.S.

I.

OBSERVATIONS ON DISEASES OF THE RECTUM. Third
Edition. 8vo. cloth, 7s. 6d.

II.

A PRACTICAL TREATISE ON DISEASES OF THE TESTIS,
SPERMATIC CORD, AND SCROTUM. Third Edition, with Engravings. 8vo. cloth, 16s.

WILLIAM DALE, M.D.LOND.

A COMPENDIUM OF PRACTICAL MEDICINE AND MORBID
ANATOMY. With Plates, 12mo. cloth, 7s.

DONALD DALRYMPLE, M.P., M.R.C.P.

THE CLIMATE OF EGYPT: METEOROLOGICAL AND MEDI-
CAL OBSERVATIONS, with Practical Hints for Invalid Travellers. Post 8vo. cloth, 4s.

JOHN DALRYMPLE, F.R.C.S., F.R.S.

PATHOLOGY OF THE HUMAN EYE. Complete in Nine Fasciculi:
imperial 4to., 20s. each; half-bound morocco, gilt tops, 9l. 15s.

HERBERT DAVIES, M.D., F.R.C.P.

ON THE PHYSICAL DIAGNOSIS OF DISEASES OF THE
LUNGS AND HEART. Second Edition. Post 8vo. cloth, 8s.

JAMES G. DAVEY, M.D., M.R.C.P.

I.

THE GANGLIONIC NERVOUS SYSTEM: its Structure, Functions,
and Diseases. 8vo. cloth, 9s.

II.

ON THE NATURE AND PROXIMATE CAUSE OF IN-
SANITY. Post 8vo. cloth, 3s.

HENRY DAY, M.D., M.R.C.P.

CLINICAL HISTORIES; with Comments. 8vo. cloth, 7s. 6d.

JAMES DIXON, F.R.C.S.

A GUIDE TO THE PRACTICAL STUDY OF DISEASES OF THE EYE. Third Edition. Post 8vo. cloth, 9s.

HORACE DOBELL, M.D.

I.

DEMONSTRATIONS OF DISEASES IN THE CHEST, AND THEIR PHYSICAL DIAGNOSIS. With Coloured Plates. 8vo. cloth, 12s. 6d.

II.

LECTURES ON THE GERMS AND VESTIGES OF DISEASE, and on the Prevention of the Invasion and Fatality of Disease by Periodical Examinations. 8vo. cloth, 6s. 6d.

III.

ON TUBERCULOSIS: ITS NATURE, CAUSE, AND TREATMENT; with Notes on Pancreatic Juice. Second Edition. Crown 8vo. cloth, 3s. 6d.

IV.

LECTURES ON WINTER COUGH (CATARRH, BRONCHITIS, EMPHYSEMA, ASTHMA); with an Appendix on some Principles of Diet in Disease. Post 8vo. cloth, 5s. 6d.

V.

LECTURES ON THE TRUE FIRST STAGE OF CONSUMPTION. Crown 8vo. cloth, 3s. 6d.

C. TOOGOOD DOWNING, M.D.

NEURALGIA: its various Forms, Pathology, and Treatment. THE JACKSONIAN PRIZE ESSAY FOR 1850. 8vo. cloth, 10s. 6d.

ROBERT DRUITT, F.R.C.S.

THE SURGEON'S VADE-MECUM; with numerous Engravings on Wood. Ninth Edition. Foolscap 8vo. cloth, 12s. 6d.

ERNEST EDWARDS, B.A.

PHOTOGRAPHS OF EMINENT MEDICAL MEN, with brief Analytical Notices of their Works. Vols. I. and II. (24 Portraits), 4to. cloth, 24s. each.

CHARLES ELAM, M.D., M.R.C.P.

MEDICINE, DISEASE, AND DEATH: being an Enquiry into the Progress of Medicine as a Practical Art. 8vo. cloth, 3s. 6d.

EDWARD ELLIS, M.D.

A PRACTICAL MANUAL OF THE DISEASES OF CHILDREN. With a Formulary. Crown 8vo. cloth, 6s.

SIR JAMES EYRE, M.D.

I.

THE STOMACH AND ITS DIFFICULTIES. Sixth Edition, by Mr. BEALE. Fcap. 8vo., 2s. 6d.

II.

PRACTICAL REMARKS ON SOME EXHAUSTING DISEASES. Second Edition. Post 8vo. cloth, 4s. 6d.

J. FAYRER, M.D., F.R.C.S., C.S.I.

CLINICAL SURGERY IN INDIA. With Engravings. 8vo. cloth, 16s.

SAMUEL FENWICK, M.D., M.R.C.P.

I.

THE MORBID STATES OF THE STOMACH AND DUO-
DENUM, AND THEIR RELATIONS TO THE DISEASES OF OTHER
ORGANS. With 10 Plates. 8vo. cloth, 12s.

II.

THE STUDENT'S GUIDE TO MEDICAL DIAGNOSIS. With
41 Engravings. Fcap. 8vo. cloth, 5s. 6d.

SIR WILLIAM FERGUSSON, BART., F.R.C.S., F.R.S.

I.

A SYSTEM OF PRACTICAL SURGERY; with numerous Illus-
trations on Wood. Fourth Edition. Fcap. 8vo. cloth, 12s. 6d.

II.

LECTURES ON THE PROGRESS OF ANATOMY AND
SURGERY DURING THE PRESENT CENTURY. With numerous Engravings.
8vo. cloth, 10s. 6d.

SIR JOHN FIFE, F.R.C.S. AND DAVID URQUHART.

MANUAL OF THE TURKISH BATH. Heat a Mode of Cure and
a Source of Strength for Men and Animals. With Engravings. Post 8vo. cloth, 5s.

W. H. FLOWER, F.R.C.S., F.R.S.

DIAGRAMS OF THE NERVES OF THE HUMAN BODY,
exhibiting their Origin, Divisions, and Connexions, with their Distribution to the various
Regions of the Cutaneous Surface, and to all the Muscles. Folio, containing Six
Plates, 14s.

WILLIAM FLUX.

THE LAW TO REGULATE THE SALE OF POISONS WITHIN
GREAT BRITAIN. Crown 8vo. cloth, 2s. 6d.

G. FOWNES, PH.D., F.R.S.

I.

A MANUAL OF CHEMISTRY; with 187 Illustrations on Wood.
Tenth Edition. Fcap. 8vo. cloth, 14s.
Edited by H. BENCE JONES, M.D., F.R.S., and HENRY WATTS, B.A., F.R.S.

II.

CHEMISTRY, AS EXEMPLIFYING THE WISDOM AND
BENEFICENCE OF GOD. Second Edition. Fcap. 8vo. cloth, 4s. 6d.

III.

INTRODUCTION TO QUALITATIVE ANALYSIS. Post 8vo. cloth, 2s.

D. J. T. FRANCIS, M.D., F.R.C.P.

CHANGE OF CLIMATE; considered as a Remedy in Dyspeptic, Pul-
monary, and other Chronic Affections; with an Account of the most Eligible Places of
Residence for Invalids, at different Seasons of the Year. Post 8vo. cloth, 8s. 6d.

W. H. FULLER, M.D., F.R.C.P.

I.

ON DISEASES OF THE LUNGS AND AIR PASSAGES.
Second Edition. 8vo. cloth, 12s. 6d.

II.

ON DISEASES OF THE HEART AND GREAT VESSELS.
8vo. cloth, 7s. 6d.

III.

ON RHEUMATISM, RHEUMATIC GOUT, AND SCIATICA:
their Pathology, Symptoms, and Treatment. Third Edition. 8vo. cloth, 12s. 6d.

REMIGIUS FRESENIUS.

A SYSTEM OF INSTRUCTION IN CHEMICAL ANALYSIS,
Edited by ARTHUR VACHER.
QUALITATIVE. Seventh Edition. 8vo. cloth, 9s.
QUANTITATIVE. Fifth Edition. 8vo. cloth, 12s. 6d.

ROBERT GALLOWAY.
I.
THE FIRST STEP IN CHEMISTRY. With numerous Engravings.
Fourth Edition. Fcap. 8vo. cloth, 6s. 6d.

II.
A KEY TO THE EXERCISES CONTAINED IN ABOVE. Fcap.
8vo., 2s. 6d.

III.
THE SECOND STEP IN CHEMISTRY; Or, the Student's Guide to
the Higher Branches of the Science. With Engravings. 8vo. cloth, 10s.

IV.
A MANUAL OF QUALITATIVE ANALYSIS. Fifth Edition.
With Engravings. Post 8vo. cloth, 8s. 6d.

V.
CHEMICAL TABLES. On Five Large Sheets, for School and Lecture
Rooms. Second Edition. 4s. 6d.

J. SAMPSON GAMGEE, M.R.C.S.
HISTORY OF A SUCCESSFUL CASE OF AMPUTATION AT
THE HIP-JOINT (the limb 48-in. in circumference, 99 pounds weight). With 4
Photographs. 4to cloth, 10s. 6d.

F. J. GANT, F.R.C.S.
I.
THE PRINCIPLES OF SURGERY: Clinical, Medical, and Opera-
tive. With Engravings. 8vo. cloth, 18s.

II.
THE IRRITABLE BLADDER: its Causes and Curative Treatment.
Second Edition, enlarged. Crown 8vo. cloth, 5s.

JOHN GAY, F.R.C.S.
ON VARICOSE DISEASE OF THE LOWER EXTREMITIES.
LETTSOMIAN LECTURES. With Plates. 8vo. cloth, 5s.

SIR DUNCAN GIBB, BART., M.D.
I.
ON DISEASES OF THE THROAT AND WINDPIPE, as
reflected by the Laryngoscope. Second Edition. With 116 Engravings. Post 8vo.
cloth, 10s. 6d.

II.
THE LARYNGOSCOPE IN DISEASES OF THE THROAT,
with a Chapter on RHINOSCOPY. Third Edition, with Engravings. Crown 8vo.,
cloth, 5s.

C. A. GORDON, M.D., C.B.
I.
ARMY HYGIENE. 8vo. cloth, 20s.

II.
CHINA, FROM A MEDICAL POINT OF VIEW: IN 1860
AND 1861; With a Chapter on Nagasaki as a Sanatarium. 8vo. cloth, 10s. 6d.

WILLIAM GAIRDNER, M.D.

ON GOUT; its History, its Causes, and its Cure. Fourth Edition. Post 8vo. cloth, 8s. 6d.

MICHAEL C. GRABHAM, M.D., M.R.C.P.

THE CLIMATE AND RESOURCES OF MADEIRA, as regarding chiefly the Necessities of Consumption and the Welfare of Invalids. With Map and Engravings. Crown 8vo. cloth, 5s.

R. J. GRAVES, M.D., F.R.S.

STUDIES IN PHYSIOLOGY AND MEDICINE. Edited by Dr. Stokes. With Portrait and Memoir. 8vo. cloth, 14s.

T. GRIFFITHS.

CHEMISTRY OF THE FOUR SEASONS — Spring, Summer, Autumn, Winter. Illustrated with Engravings on Wood. Second Edition. Foolscap 8vo. cloth, 7s. 6d.

JAMES M. GULLY, M.D.

THE SIMPLE TREATMENT OF DISEASE; deduced from the Methods of Expectancy and Revulsion. 18mo. cloth, 4s.

W. A. GUY, M.B., F.R.S., AND JOHN HARLEY, M.D., F.R.C.P.

HOOPER'S PHYSICIAN'S VADE-MECUM; OR, MANUAL OF THE PRINCIPLES AND PRACTICE OF PHYSIC. Seventh Edition. With Engravings. Foolscap 8vo. cloth, 12s. 6d.

GUY'S HOSPITAL REPORTS. Third Series. Vol. XV., 8vo. 7s. 6d.

S. O. HABERSHON, M.D., F.R.C.P.

I.

ON DISEASES OF THE ABDOMEN, comprising those of the Stomach and other Parts of the Alimentary Canal, Œsophagus, Stomach, Cæcum, Intestines, and Peritoneum. Second Edition, with Plates. 8vo. cloth, 14s.

II.

ON THE INJURIOUS EFFECTS OF MERCURY IN THE TREATMENT OF DISEASE. Post 8vo. cloth, 3s. 6d.

C. RADCLYFFE HALL, F.R.C.P.

TORQUAY IN ITS MEDICAL ASPECT AS A RESORT FOR PULMONARY INVALIDS. Post 8vo. cloth, 5s.

MARSHALL HALL, M.D., F.R.S.

I.

PRONE AND POSTURAL RESPIRATION IN DROWNING AND OTHER FORMS OF APNŒA OR SUSPENDED RESPIRATION. Post 8vo. cloth, 5s.

II.

PRACTICAL OBSERVATIONS AND SUGGESTIONS IN MEDICINE. Second Series. Post 8vo. cloth, 8s. 6d.

REV. T F. HARDWICH.

A MANUAL OF PHOTOGRAPHIC CHEMISTRY. With Engravings. Seventh Edition. Foolscap 8vo. cloth, 7s. 6d.

J. BOWER HARRISON, M.D., M.R.C.P.

I.

LETTERS TO A YOUNG PRACTITIONER ON THE DIS-EASES OF CHILDREN. Foolscap 8vo. cloth, 3s.

II.

ON THE CONTAMINATION OF WATER BY THE POISON OF LEAD, and its Effects on the Human Body. Foolscap 8vo. cloth, 3s. 6d.

GEORGE HARTWIG, M.D.

I.

ON SEA BATHING AND SEA AIR. Second Edition. Fcap. 8vo., 2s. 6d.

II.

ON THE PHYSICAL EDUCATION OF CHILDREN. Fcap. 8vo., 2s. 6d.

A. H. HASSALL, M.D.

THE URINE, IN HEALTH AND DISEASE; being an Explanation of the Composition of the Urine, and of the Pathology and Treatment of Urinary and Renal Disorders. Second Edition. With 79 Engravings (23 Coloured). Post 8vo. cloth, 12s. 6d.

ALFRED HAVILAND, M.R.C.S.

CLIMATE, WEATHER, AND DISEASE; being a Sketch of the Opinions of the most celebrated Ancient and Modern Writers with regard to the Influence of Climate and Weather in producing Disease. With Four coloured Engravings. 8vo. cloth, 7s.

W. HAYCOCK, M.R.C.V.S.

HORSES; HOW THEY OUGHT TO BE SHOD: being a plain and practical Treatise on the Principles and Practice of the Farrier's Art. With 14 Plates. Cloth, 7s. 6d.

F. W. HEADLAND, M.D., F.R.C.P.

I.

ON THE ACTION OF MEDICINES IN THE SYSTEM. Fourth Edition. 8vo. cloth, 14s.

II.

A MEDICAL HANDBOOK; comprehending such Information on Medical and Sanitary Subjects as is desirable in Educated Persons. Second Thousand. Foolscap 8vo. cloth, 5s.

J. N. HEALE, M.D., M.R.C.P.

I.

A TREATISE ON THE PHYSIOLOGICAL ANATOMY OF THE LUNGS. With Engravings. 8vo. cloth, 8s.

II.

A TREATISE ON VITAL CAUSES. 8vo. cloth, 9s.

CHRISTOPHER HEATH, F.R.C.S.

I.

PRACTICAL ANATOMY: a Manual of Dissections. With numerous Engravings. Second Edition. Fcap. 8vo. cloth, 12s. 6d.

II.

A MANUAL OF MINOR SURGERY AND BANDAGING, FOR THE USE OF HOUSE-SURGEONS, DRESSERS, AND JUNIOR PRACTITIONERS. With Illustrations. Third Edition. Fcap. 8vo. cloth, 5s.

III.

INJURIES AND DISEASES OF THE JAWS. JACKSONIAN PRIZE ESSAY. With Engravings. 8vo. cloth, 12s.

JOHN HIGGINBOTTOM, F.R.S., F.R.C.S.E.

A PRACTICAL ESSAY ON THE USE OF THE NITRATE OF SILVER IN THE TREATMENT OF INFLAMMATION, WOUNDS, AND ULCERS. Third Edition, 8vo. cloth, 6s.

WILLIAM HINDS, M.D.

THE HARMONIES OF PHYSICAL SCIENCE IN RELATION TO THE HIGHER SENTIMENTS; with Observations on Medical Studies, and on the Moral and Scientific Relations of Medical Life. Post 8vo. cloth, 4s.

J. A. HINGESTON, M.R.C.S.

TOPICS OF THE DAY, MEDICAL, SOCIAL, AND SCIENTIFIC. Crown 8vo. cloth, 7s. 6d.

RICHARD HODGES, M.D.

THE NATURE, PATHOLOGY, AND TREATMENT OF PUERPERAL CONVULSIONS. Crown 8vo. cloth, 3s.

DECIMUS HODGSON, M.D.

THE PROSTATE GLAND, AND ITS ENLARGEMENT IN OLD AGE. With 12 Plates. Royal 8vo. cloth, 6s.

JABEZ HOGG, M.R.C.S.

A MANUAL OF OPHTHALMOSCOPIC SURGERY; being a Practical Treatise on the Use of the Ophthalmoscope in Diseases of the Eye. Third Edition. With Coloured Plates. 8vo. cloth, 10s. 6d.

LUTHER HOLDEN, F.R.C.S.

I.

HUMAN OSTEOLOGY: with Plates, showing the Attachments of the Muscles. Fourth Edition. 8vo. cloth, 16s.

II.

A MANUAL OF THE DISSECTION OF THE HUMAN BODY. With Engravings on Wood. Third Edition. 8vo. cloth, 16s.

BARNARD HOLT, F.R.C.S.

ON THE IMMEDIATE TREATMENT OF STRICTURE OF THE URETHRA. Third Edition, Enlarged. 8vo. cloth, 6s.

SIR CHARLES HOOD, M.D.

SUGGESTIONS FOR THE FUTURE PROVISION OF CRIMI-

NAL LUNATICS. 8vo. cloth, 5s. 6d.

P. HOOD M.D.

THE SUCCESSFUL TREATMENT OF SCARLET FEVER;

also, OBSERVATIONS ON THE PATHOLOGY AND TREATMENT OF
CROWING INSPIRATIONS OF INFANTS. Post 8vo. cloth, 5s.

JOHN HORSLEY.

A CATECHISM OF CHEMICAL PHILOSOPHY; being a Familiar

Exposition of the Principles of Chemistry and Physics. With Engravings on Wood.
Designed for the Use of Schools and Private Teachers. Post 8vo. cloth, 6s. 6d.

JAMES A. HORTON, M.D.

PHYSICAL AND MEDICAL CLIMATE AND METEOROLOGY

OF THE WEST COAST OF AFRICA. 8vo. cloth, 10s.

LUKE HOWARD, F.R.S.

ESSAY ON THE MODIFICATIONS OF CLOUDS. Third Edition,

by W. D. and E. HOWARD. With 6 Lithographic Plates, from Pictures by Kenyon.
4to. cloth, 10s. 6d.

A. HAMILTON HOWE, M.D.

A THEORETICAL INQUIRY INTO THE PHYSICAL CAUSE

OF EPIDEMIC DISEASES. Accompanied with Tables. 8vo. cloth, 7s.

C. W. HUFELAND.

THE ART OF PROLONGING LIFE. Second Edition. Edited

by ERASMUS WILSON, F.R.S. Foolscap 8vo., 2s. 6d.

W. CURTIS HUGMAN, F.R.C.S.

ON HIP-JOINT DISEASE; with reference especially to Treatment

by Mechanical Means for the Relief of Contraction and Deformity of the Affected Limb.
With Plates. Re-issue, enlarged. 8vo. cloth, 3s. 6d.

J. W. HULKE, F.R.C.S., F.R.S.

A PRACTICAL TREATISE ON THE USE OF THE

OPHTHALMOSCOPE. Being the Jacksonian Prize Essay for 1859. Royal 8vo.
cloth, 8s.

HENRY HUNT, F.R.C.P.

ON HEARTBURN AND INDIGESTION. 8vo. cloth, 5s.

G. Y. HUNTER, M.R.C.S.

BODY AND MIND : the Nervous System and its Derangements.

Fcap. 8vo. cloth, 3s. 6d.

JONATHAN HUTCHINSON, F.R.C.S.

A CLINICAL MEMOIR ON CERTAIN DISEASES OF THE
EYE AND EAR, CONSEQUENT ON INHERITED SYPHILIS; with an
appended Chapter of Commentaries on the Transmission of Syphilis from Parent to
Offspring, and its more remote Consequences. With Plates and Woodcuts, 8vo. cloth, 9s.

T. H. HUXLEY, LL.D., F.R.S.

INTRODUCTION TO THE CLASSIFICATION OF ANIMALS.
With Engravings. 8vo. cloth, 6s.

THOMAS INMAN, M.D., M.R.C.P.

I.

ON MYALGIA: ITS NATURE, CAUSES, AND TREATMENT;
being a Treatise on Painful and other Affections of the Muscular System. Second
Edition. 8vo. cloth, 9s.

II.

FOUNDATION FOR A NEW THEORY AND PRACTICE
OF MEDICINE. Second Edition. Crown 8vo. cloth, 10s.

JAMES JAGO, M.D.OXON., A.B.CANTAB.

ENTOPTICS, WITH ITS USES IN PHYSIOLOGY AND
MEDICINE. With 54 Engravings. Crown 8vo. cloth, 5s.

M. PROSSER JAMES, M.D., M.R.C.P.

SORE-THROAT: ITS NATURE, VARIETIES, AND TREAT-
MENT; including the Use of the LARYNGOSCOPE as an Aid to Diagnosis. Second
Edition, with numerous Engravings. Post 8vo. cloth, 5s.

F. E. JENCKEN, M.D., M.R.C.P.

THE CHOLERA: ITS ORIGIN, IDIOSYNCRACY, AND
TREATMENT. Fcap. 8vo. cloth, 2s. 6d.

C. HANDFIELD JONES, M.B., F.R.C.P., F.R.S.

STUDIES ON FUNCTIONAL NERVOUS DISORDERS. Second
Edition, much enlarged. 8vo. cloth, 18s.

H. BENCE JONES, M.D., F.R.C.P., F.R.S.

I.

LECTURES ON SOME OF THE APPLICATIONS OF
CHEMISTRY AND MECHANICS TO PATHOLOGY AND THERA-
PEUTICS. 8vo. cloth, 12s.

II.

CROONIAN LECTURES ON MATTER AND FORCE. Fcap. 8vo.
cloth, 5s.

C. HANDFIELD JONES, M.B., F.R.S., & E. H. SIEVEKING, M.D., F.R.C.P.

A MANUAL OF PATHOLOGICAL ANATOMY. Illustrated with
numerous Engravings on Wood. Foolscap 8vo. cloth, 12s. 6d.

JAMES JONES, M.D., M.R.C.P.

ON THE USE OF PERCHLORIDE OF IRON AND OTHER
CHALYBEATE SALTS IN THE TREATMENT OF CONSUMPTION. Crown
8vo. cloth, 3s. 6d.

T. WHARTON JONES, F.R.C.S., F.R.S.

I.

A MANUAL OF THE PRINCIPLES AND PRACTICE OF
OPHTHALMIC MEDICINE AND SURGERY; with Nine Coloured Plates and
173 Wood Engravings. Third Edition, thoroughly revised. Foolscap 8vo. cloth, 12s. 6d.

II.

THE WISDOM AND BENEFICENCE OF THE ALMIGHTY,
AS DISPLAYED IN THE SENSE OF VISION. Actonian Prize Essay. With
Illustrations on Steel and Wood. Foolscap 8vo. cloth, 4s. 6d.

III.

DEFECTS OF SIGHT AND HEARING : their Nature, Causes, Pre-
vention, and General Management. Second Edition, with Engravings. Fcap. 8vo. 2s. 6d.

IV.

A CATECHISM OF THE MEDICINE AND SURGERY OF
THE EYE AND EAR. For the Clinical Use of Hospital Students. Fcap. 8vo. 2s. 6d.

V.

A CATECHISM OF THE PHYSIOLOGY AND PHILOSOPHY
OF BODY, SENSE, AND MIND. For Use in Schools and Colleges. Fcap. 8vo.,
2s. 6d.

U. J. KAY-SHUTTLEWORTH, M.P.

FIRST PRINCIPLES OF MODERN CHEMISTRY : a Manual
of Inorganic Chemistry. Second Edition. Crown 8vo. cloth, 4s. 6d.

DR. LAENNEC.

A MANUAL OF AUSCULTATION AND PERCUSSION. Trans-
lated and Edited by J. B. Sharpe, M.R.C.S. 3s.

SIR WM. LAWRENCE, BART., F.R.S.

I.

LECTURES ON SURGERY. 8vo. cloth, 16s.

II.

A TREATISE ON RUPTURES. The Fifth Edition, considerably
enlarged. 8vo. cloth, 16s.

ARTHUR LEARED, M.D., M.R.C.P.

IMPERFECT DIGESTION : ITS CAUSES AND TREATMENT.
Fifth Edition. Foolscap 8vo. cloth, 4s. 6d.

HENRY LEE, F.R.C.S.

PRACTICAL PATHOLOGY. Third Edition, in 2 Vols. Containing
Lectures on Suppurative Fever, Diseases of the Veins, Hæmorrhoidal Tumours, Diseases
of the Rectum, Syphilis, Gonorrhœal Ophthalmia, &c. 8vo. cloth, 10s. each vol.

EDWIN LEE, M.D.

I.

THE EFFECT OF CLIMATE ON TUBERCULOUS DISEASE,
with Notices of the chief Foreign Places of Winter Resort. Small 8vo. cloth, 4s. 6d.

II.

THE WATERING PLACES OF ENGLAND, CONSIDERED
with Reference to their Medical Topography. Fourth Edition. Fcap. 8vo. cloth, 7s. 6d.

III.

THE BATHS OF FRANCE. Fourth Edition. Fcap. 8vo. cloth,
4s. 6d.

IV.

THE BATHS OF GERMANY. Fourth Edition. Post 8vo. cloth, 7s.

V.

THE BATHS OF SWITZERLAND. 12mo. cloth, 3s. 6d.

VI.

HOMŒOPATHY AND HYDROPATHY IMPARTIALLY AP-
PRECIATED. Fourth Edition. Post 8vo. cloth, 3s.

ROBERT LEE, M.D, F.R.C.P., F.R.S.

I.

CONSULTATIONS IN MIDWIFERY. Foolscap 8vo. cloth, 4s. 6d.

II.

A TREATISE ON THE SPECULUM; with Three Hundred Cases.
8vo. cloth, 4s. 6d.

III.

CLINICAL REPORTS OF OVARIAN AND UTERINE DIS-
EASES, with Commentaries. Foolscap 8vo. cloth, 6s. 6d.

IV.

CLINICAL MIDWIFERY: comprising the Histories of 545 Cases of
Difficult, Preternatural, and Complicated Labour, with Commentaries. Second Edition.
Foolscap 8vo. cloth, 5s.

WM. LEISHMAN, M.D., F.F.P.S.

THE MECHANISM OF PARTURITION: An Essay, Historical and
Critical. With Engravings. 8vo. cloth, 5s.

F. HARWOOD LESCHER.

THE ELEMENTS OF PHARMACY. 8vo. cloth, 7s. 6d.

ROBERT LISTON, F.R.S.

PRACTICAL SURGERY. Fourth Edition. 8vo. cloth, 22s.

D. D. LOGAN, M.D., M.R.C.P.LOND.

ON OBSTINATE DISEASES OF THE SKIN. Fcap.8vo.cloth,2s.6d.

LONDON HOSPITAL.

CLINICAL LECTURES AND REPORTS BY THE MEDICAL
AND SURGICAL STAFF. With Illustrations. Vols. I. to IV. 8vo. cloth, 7s. 6d.

LONDON MEDICAL SOCIETY OF OBSERVATION.

WHAT TO OBSERVE AT THE BED-SIDE, AND AFTER
DEATH. Published by Authority. Second Edition. Foolscap 8vo. cloth, 4s. 6d.

HENRY LOWNDES, M.R.C.S.

AN ESSAY ON THE MAINTENANCE OF HEALTH. Fcap.
8vo. cloth, 2s. 6d.

MORELL MACKENZIE, M.D. LOND., M.R.C.P.

HOARSENESS, LOSS OF VOICE, AND STRIDULOUS
BREATHING in relation to NERVO-MUSCULAR AFFECTIONS of the
LARYNX. Second Edition. Fully Illustrated. 8vo. 2s. 6d.

DANIEL MACLACHLAN, M.D., F.R.C.P.L.

THE DISEASES AND INFIRMITIES OF ADVANCED LIFE.
8vo. cloth, 16s.

A. C. MACLEOD, M.R.C.P.LOND.

ACHOLIC DISEASES ; comprising Jaundice, Diarrhœa, Dysentery,
and Cholera. Post 8vo. cloth, 5s. 6d.

GEORGE H. B. MACLEOD, M.D., F.R.C.S.EDIN.

I.

OUTLINES OF SURGICAL DIAGNOSIS. 8vo. cloth, 12s. 6d.

II.

NOTES ON THE SURGERY OF THE CRIMEAN WAR; with
REMARKS on GUN-SHOT WOUNDS. 8vo. cloth, 10s. 6d.

WM. MACLEOD, M.D., F.R.C.P.EDIN.

THE THEORY OF THE TREATMENT OF DISEASE ADOPTED
AT BEN RHYDDING. Fcap. 8vo. cloth, 2s. 6d.

JOSEPH MACLISE, F.R.C.S.

I.

SURGICAL ANATOMY. A Series of Dissections, illustrating the Prin-
cipal Regions of the Human Body. Second Edition, folio, cloth, £3. 12s.; half-morocco,
£4. 4s.

II.

ON DISLOCATIONS AND FRACTURES. This Work is Uniform
with "Surgical Anatomy;" folio, cloth, £2. 10s.; half-morocco, £2. 17s.

N. C. MACNAMARA.

I.

A MANUAL OF THE DISEASES OF THE EYE. With
Coloured Plates. Fcap. 8vo. cloth, 12s. 6d.

II.

A TREATISE ON ASIATIC CHOLERA; with Maps. 8vo. cloth,
16s.

WM. MARCET, M.D., F.R.C.P., F.R.S.

ON CHRONIC ALCOHOLIC INTOXICATION; with an INQUIRY
INTO THE INFLUENCE OF THE ABUSE OF ALCOHOL AS A PRE-
DISPOSING CAUSE OF DISEASE. Second Edition, much enlarged. Foolscap
8vo. cloth, 4s. 6d.

J. MACPHERSON, M.D.

CHOLERA IN ITS HOME; with a Sketch of the Pathology and Treatment of the Disease. Crown 8vo. cloth, 5s.

W. O. MARKHAM, M.D., F.R.C.P.

I.

DISEASES OF THE HEART: THEIR PATHOLOGY, DIAG-NOSIS, AND TREATMENT. Second Edition. Post 8vo. cloth, 6s.

II.

SKODA ON AUSCULTATION AND PERCUSSION. Post 8vo. cloth, 6s.

III.

BLEEDING AND CHANGE IN TYPE OF DISEASES. Gulstonian Lectures for 1864. Crown 8vo. 2s. 6d.

ALEXANDER MARSDEN, M.D., F.R.C.S.

A NEW AND SUCCESSFUL MODE OF TREATING CERTAIN FORMS OF CANCER; to which is prefixed a Practical and Systematic Description of all the Varieties of this Disease. With Coloured Plates. 8vo. cloth, 6s. 6d.

SIR RANALD MARTIN, C.B., F.R.C.S., F.R.S.

INFLUENCE OF TROPICAL CLIMATES IN PRODUCING THE ACUTE ENDEMIC DISEASES OF EUROPEANS; including Practical Observations on their Chronic Sequelæ under the Influences of the Climate of Europe. Second Edition, much enlarged. 8vo. cloth, 20s.

P. MARTYN, M.D.LOND.

HOOPING-COUGH; ITS PATHOLOGY AND TREATMENT. With Engravings. 8vo. cloth, 2s. 6d.

C. F. MAUNDER, F.R.C.S.

OPERATIVE SURGERY. With 158 Engravings. Post 8vo. 6s.

R. G. MAYNE, M.D., LL.D.

I.

AN EXPOSITORY LEXICON OF THE TERMS, ANCIENT AND MODERN, IN MEDICAL AND GENERAL SCIENCE. 8vo. cloth, £2. 10s.

II.

A MEDICAL VOCABULARY; or, an Explanation of all Names, Synonymes, Terms, and Phrases used in Medicine and the relative branches of Medical Science. Third Edition. Fcap. 8vo. cloth, 8s. 6d.

EDWARD MERYON, M.D., F.R.C.P.

PATHOLOGICAL AND PRACTICAL RESEARCHES ON THE VARIOUS FORMS OF PARALYSIS. 8vo. cloth, 6s.

W. J. MOORE, M.D.

I.

HEALTH IN THE TROPICS; or, Sanitary Art applied to Europeans in India. 8vo. cloth, 9s.

II.

A MANUAL OF THE DISEASES OF INDIA. Fcap. 8vo. cloth, 5s.

JAMES MORRIS, M.D.LOND.

I.

GERMINAL MATTER AND THE CONTACT THEORY:

An Essay on the Morbid Poisons. Second Edition. Crown 8vo. cloth, 4s. 6d.

II.

IRRITABILITY: Popular and Practical Sketches of Common Morbid States

and Conditions bordering on Disease; with Hints for Management, Alleviation, and Cure. Crown 8vo. cloth, 4s. 6d.

G. J. MULDER.

THE CHEMISTRY OF WINE. Edited by H. Bence Jones, M.D.,

F.R.S. Fcap. 8vo. cloth, 6s.

W. MURRAY, M.D., M.R.C.P.

EMOTIONAL DISORDERS OF THE SYMPATHETIC SYS-

TEM OF NERVES. Crown 8vo. cloth, 3s. 6d.

W. B. MUSHET, M.B., M.R.C.P.

ON APOPLEXY, AND ALLIED AFFECTIONS OF THE

BRAIN. 8vo. cloth, 7s.

GEORGE NAYLER, F.R.C.S.

ON THE DISEASES OF THE SKIN. With Plates. 8vo. cloth,

10s. 6d.

J. BIRKBECK NEVINS, M.D.

THE PRESCRIBER'S ANALYSIS OF THE BRITISH PHAR-

MACOPEIA of 1867. 32mo. cloth, 3s. 6d.

H. M. NOAD, PH.D., F.R.S.

THE INDUCTION COIL, being a Popular Explanation of the Electrical

Principles on which it is constructed. Third Edition. With Engravings. Fcap. 8vo. cloth, 3s.

DANIEL NOBLE, M.D., F.R.C.P.

THE HUMAN MIND IN ITS RELATIONS WITH THE

BRAIN AND NERVOUS SYSTEM. Post 8vo. cloth, 4s. 6d.

SELBY NORTON, M.D.

INFANTILE DISEASES: their Causes, Prevention, and Treatment,

showing by what Means the present Mortality may be greatly reduced. Fcap. 8vo. cloth, 2s. 6d.

THOMAS NUNNELEY, F.R.C.S.

I.

ON THE ORGANS OF VISION: THEIR ANATOMY AND PHY-

SIOLOGY. With Plates, 8vo. cloth, 15s.

II.

A TREATISE ON THE NATURE, CAUSES, AND TREATMENT

OF ERYSIPELAS. 8vo. cloth, 10s. 6d.

FRANCIS OPPERT, M.D., M.R.C.P.

I.

HOSPITALS, INFIRMARIES, AND DISPENSARIES; their

Construction, Interior Arrangement, and Management, with Descriptions of existing Institutions. With 58 Engravings. Royal 8vo. cloth, 10s. 6d.

II.

VISCERAL AND HEREDITARY SYPHILIS. 8vo. cloth, 5s.

LANGSTON PARKER, F.R.C.S.

THE MODERN TREATMENT OF SYPHILITIC DISEASES,

both Primary and Secondary; comprising the Treatment of Constitutional and Confirmed Syphilis, by a safe and successful Method. Fourth Edition. 8vo. cloth, 10s.

E. A. PARKES, M.D., F.R.C.P., F.R.S.

I.

A MANUAL OF PRACTICAL HYGIENE; intended especially for
the Medical Officers of the Army. With Plates and Woodcuts. 3rd Edition, 8vo. cloth, 16s.

II.

THE URINE: ITS COMPOSITION IN HEALTH AND DISEASE,
AND UNDER THE ACTION OF REMEDIES. 8vo. cloth, 12s.

JOHN PARKIN, M.D., F.R.C.S.

I.

THE ANTIDOTAL TREATMENT AND PREVENTION OF
THE EPIDEMIC CHOLERA. Third Edition. 8vo. cloth, 7s. 6d.

II.

THE CAUSATION AND PREVENTION OF DISEASE; with
the Laws regulating the Extrication of Malaria from the Surface, and its Diffusion in the surrounding Air. 8vo. cloth, 5s.

JAMES PART, F.R.C.S.

THE MEDICAL AND SURGICAL POCKET CASE BOOK,
for the Registration of important Cases in Private Practice, and to assist the Student of Hospital Practice. Second Edition. 2s. 6d.

JOHN PATTERSON, M.D.

EGYPT AND THE NILE AS A WINTER RESORT FOR
PULMONARY AND OTHER INVALIDS. Fcap. 8vo. cloth, 3s.

F. W. PAVY, M.D., F.R.S., F.R.C.P.

I.

DIABETES : RESEARCHES ON ITS NATURE AND TREAT-
MENT. Second Edition. With Engravings. 8vo. cloth, 10s.

II.

DIGESTION : ITS DISORDERS AND THEIR TREATMENT.
Second Edition. 8vo. cloth, 8s. 6d.

T. B. PEACOCK, M.D., F.R.C.P.

I.

ON MALFORMATIONS OF THE HUMAN HEART. With
Original Cases and Illustrations. Second Edition. With 8 Plates. 8vo. cloth, 10s.

II.

ON SOME OF THE CAUSES AND EFFECTS OF VALVULAR
DISEASE OF THE HEART. With Engravings. 8vo. cloth, 5s.

W. H. PEARSE, M.D.EDIN.

NOTES ON HEALTH IN CALCUTTA AND BRITISH
EMIGRANT SHIPS, including Ventilation, Diet, and Disease. Fcap. 8vo. 2s.

JONATHAN PEREIRA, M.D., F.R.S.

SELECTA E PRÆSCRIPTIS. Fifteenth Edition. 24mo. cloth, 5s.

JAMES H. PICKFORD, M.D.

HYGIENE; or, Health as Depending upon the Conditions of the Atmo-
sphere, Food and Drinks, Motion and Rest, Sleep and Wakefulness, Secretions, Excretions, and Retentions, Mental Emotions, Clothing, Bathing, &c. Vol. I. 8vo. cloth, 9s.

WILLIAM PIRRIE, M.D., C.M., F.R.S.E.

THE PRINCIPLES AND PRACTICE OF SURGERY. With
numerous Engravings on Wood. Second Edition. 8vo. cloth, 24s.

WILLIAM PIRRIE, M.D.

ON HAY ASTHMA, AND THE AFFECTION TERMED
HAY FEVER. Fcap. 8vo. cloth, 2s. 6d.

HENRY POWER, F.R.C.S., M.B.LOND.

ILLUSTRATIONS OF SOME OF THE PRINCIPAL DISEASES
OF THE EYE: With an Account of their Symptoms, Pathology and Treatment.
Twelve Coloured Plates. 8vo. cloth, 20s.

HENRY F. A. PRATT, M.D., M.R.C.P.

I.

THE GENEALOGY OF CREATION, newly Translated from the
Unpointed Hebrew Text of the Book of Genesis, showing the General Scientific Accuracy
of the Cosmogony of Moses and the Philosophy of Creation. 8vo. cloth, 14s.

II.

ON ECCENTRIC AND CENTRIC FORCE: A New Theory of
Projection. With Engravings. 8vo. cloth, 10s.

III.

ON ORBITAL MOTION: The Outlines of a System of Physical
Astronomy. With Diagrams. 8vo. cloth, 7s. 6d.

IV.

ASTRONOMICAL INVESTIGATIONS. The Cosmical Relations of
the Revolution of the Lunar Apsides. Oceanic Tides. With Engravings. 8vo. cloth, 5s.

V.

THE ORACLES OF GOD: An Attempt at a Re-interpretation. Part I.
The Revealed Cosmos. 8vo. cloth, 10s.

THE PRESCRIBER'S PHARMACOPŒIA; containing all the Medi-
cines in the British Pharmacopœia, arranged in Classes according to their Action, with
their Composition and Doses. By a Practising Physician. Fifth Edition. 32mo.
cloth, 2s. 6d.; roan tuck (for the pocket), 3s. 6d.

JOHN ROWLISON PRETTY, M.D.

AIDS DURING LABOUR, including the Administration of Chloroform,
the Management of Placenta and Post-partum Hæmorrhage. Fcap. 8vo. cloth, 4s. 6d.

P. C. PRICE, F.R.C.S.

AN ESSAY ON EXCISION OF THE KNEE-JOINT. With
Coloured Plates. With Memoir of the Author and Notes by Henry Smith, F.R.C.S.
Royal 8vo. cloth, 14s.

PHOTOGRAPHIC MANIPULATION : A Manual treating of the
Practice of the Art, and its various Applications to Nature. With numerous Engravings.
Second Edition. Crown 8vo. cloth, 6s. 6d.

LECTURES ON THE DEVELOPMENT OF THE GRAVID
UTERUS. 8vo. cloth, 5s. 6d.

ON THE MODE OF FORMATION OF SHELLS OF ANIMALS,
OF BONE, AND OF SEVERAL OTHER STRUCTURES, by a Process of
Molecular Coalescence, Demonstrable in certain Artificially-formed Products. Fcap. 8vo.
cloth, 4s. 6d.

DEFORMITIES OF THE MOUTH, CONGENITAL AND
ACCIDENTAL : Their Mechanical Treatment. With Illustrations. 8vo. cloth, 5s.

THE PRINCIPLES AND PRACTICE OF OBSTETRIC MEDI-
CINE AND SURGERY. Illustrated with One Hundred and Twenty Plates on Steel
and Wood; forming one thick handsome volume. Fifth Edition. 8vo. cloth, 22s.

SYPHILITIC AFFECTIONS OF THE NERVOUS SYSTEM,
AND A CASE OF SYMMETRICAL MUSCULAR ATROPHY ; with other
Contributions to the Pathology of the Spinal Marrow. Post 8vo. cloth, 5s.

A SUPPLEMENT TO THE PHARMACOPŒIA : A concise but
comprehensive Dispensatory, and Manual of Facts and Formulæ, for the use of Practitioners in Medicine and Pharmacy. Third Edition. 8vo. cloth, 22s.

ANIMAL ELECTRICITY ; Edited by H. BENCE JONES, M.D., F.R.S.
With Fifty Engravings on Wood. Foolscap 8vo. cloth, 6s.

I.
EPILEPSY: ITS SYMPTOMS, TREATMENT, AND RELATION
TO OTHER CHRONIC CONVULSIVE DISEASES. 8vo. cloth, 10s.
II.
THE DIAGNOSIS OF DISEASES OF THE BRAIN, SPINAL
CORD, AND THEIR APPENDAGES. 8vo. cloth, 8s.

ON THE CAUSE OF THE COAGULATION OF THE BLOOD.
Being the ASTLEY COOPER PRIZE ESSAY for 1856. With a Practical Appendix.
8vo. cloth, 16s.

WILLIAM ROBERTS, M.D., F.R.C.P.

AN ESSAY ON WASTING PALSY; being a Systematic Treatise on the Disease hitherto described as ATROPHIE MUSCULAIRE PROGRESSIVE. With Four Plates. 8vo. cloth, 5s.

C. H. F. ROUTH, D.M., M.R.C.P.

INFANT FEEDING, AND ITS INFLUENCE ON LIFE; Or, the Causes and Prevention of Infant Mortality. Second Edition. Fcap. 8vo. cloth, 6s.

W. H. ROBERTSON, M.D., M.R.C.P.

I.
THE NATURE AND TREATMENT OF GOUT. 8vo. cloth, 10s. 6d.

II.
A TREATISE ON DIET AND REGIMEN. Fourth Edition. 2 vols. 12s. post 8vo. cloth.

JAMES ROGERS, M.D.

ON THE PRESENT STATE OF THERAPEUTICS. With some Suggestions for placing it on a more scientific basis. 8vo. cloth, 6s. 6d.

JAMES ROGERS, M.D.

ON THE PRESENT STATE OF THERAPEUTICS. With some Suggestions for placing it on a more scientific basis. 8vo. cloth, 6s. 6d.

G. R. ROWE, M.D.

NERVOUS DISEASES, LIVER AND STOMACH COM-PLAINTS, LOW SPIRITS, INDIGESTION, GOUT, ASTHMA, AND DIS-ORDERS PRODUCED BY TROPICAL CLIMATES. With Cases. Sixteenth Edition. Fcap. 8vo. 2s. 6d.

J. F. ROYLE, M.D., F.R.S., AND F. W. HEADLAND, M.D., F.R.C.P.

A MANUAL OF MATERIA MEDICA AND THERAPEUTICS. With numerous Engravings on Wood. Fifth Edition. Fcap. 8vo. cloth, 12s. 6d.

W. B. RYAN, M.D.

INFANTICIDE: ITS LAW, PREVALENCE, PREVENTION, AND HISTORY. 8vo. cloth, 5s.

ST. GEORGE'S HOSPITAL REPORTS. Vols. I. to IV. 8vo. 7s. 6d.

T. P. SALT, BIRMINGHAM.

ON DEFORMITIES AND DEBILITIES OF THE LOWER EXTREMITIES AND THE MECHANICAL TREATMENT EMPLOYED IN THE PROMOTION OF THEIR CURE. With Plates. 8vo. cloth, 15s.

H. HYDE SALTER, M.D., F.R.C.P., F.R.S.

ASTHMA. Second Edition. 8vo. cloth, 10s.

W. H. O. SANKEY, M.D.LOND.

LECTURES ON MENTAL DISEASES. 8vo. cloth, 8s.

A. E. SANSOM, M.D.LOND., M.R.C.P.

I.

CHLOROFORM: ITS ACTION AND ADMINISTRATION. A Hand-
book. With Engravings. Crown 8vo. cloth, 5s.

II.

THE ARREST AND PREVENTION OF CHOLERA; being a
Guide to the Antiseptic Treatment. Fcap. 8vo. cloth, 2s. 6d.

JOHN SAVORY, M.S.A.

A COMPENDIUM OF DOMESTIC MEDICINE, AND COMPA-
NION TO THE MEDICINE CHEST; intended as a Source of Easy Reference for
Clergymen, and for Families residing at a Distance from Professional Assistance.
Seventh Edition. 12mo. cloth, 5s.

HERMANN SCHACHT.

THE MICROSCOPE, AND ITS APPLICATION TO VEGETABLE
ANATOMY AND PHYSIOLOGY. Edited by FREDERICK CURREY, M.A. Post
8vo. cloth, 6s.

R. E. SCORESBY-JACKSON, M.D., F.R.S.E.

MEDICAL CLIMATOLOGY; or, a Topographical and Meteorological
Description of the Localities resorted to in Winter and Summer by Invalids of various
classes both at Home and Abroad. With an Isothermal Chart. Post 8vo. cloth, 12s.

R. H. SEMPLE M.D., M.R.C.P.

ON COUGH: its Causes, Varieties, and Treatment. With some practical
Remarks on the Use of the Stethoscope as an aid to Diagnosis. Post 8vo. cloth, 4s. 6d.

E. J. SEYMOUR, M.D.

I.

ILLUSTRATIONS OF SOME OF THE PRINCIPAL DIS-
EASES OF THE OVARIA: their Symptoms and Treatment; to which are prefixed
Observations on the Structure and Functions of those parts in the Human Being and in
Animals. On India paper. Folio, 16s.

II.

THE NATURE AND TREATMENT OF DROPSY; considered
especially in reference to the Diseases of the Internal Organs of the Body, which most
commonly produce it. 8vo. 5s.

THOS. SHAPTER, M.D., F.R.C.P.

THE CLIMATE OF THE SOUTH OF DEVON, AND ITS
INFLUENCE UPON HEALTH. Second Edition, with Maps. 8vo. cloth, 10s. 6d.

E. SHAW, M.R.C.S.

THE MEDICAL REMEMBRANCER; OR, BOOK OF EMER-
GENCIES. Fifth Edition. Edited, with Additions, by JONATHAN HUTCHINSON, F.R.C.S.
32mo. cloth, 2s. 6d.

JOHN SHEA, M.D., B.A.

A MANUAL OF ANIMAL PHYSIOLOGY With an Appendix of
Questions for the B.A. London and other Examinations. With Engravings. Foolscap
8vo. cloth, 5s. 6d.

CHARLES SHRIMPTON, M.D.

CHOLERA: ITS SEAT, NATURE, AND TREATMENT. With
Engravings. 8vo. cloth, 4s. 6d.

FRANCIS SIBSON, M.D., F.R.C.P., F.R.S.

MEDICAL ANATOMY. With coloured Plates. Imperial folio. Complete in Seven Fasciculi. 5s. each.

E. H. SIEVEKING, M.D., F.R.C.P.

ON EPILEPSY AND EPILEPTIFORM SEIZURES: their Causes, Pathology, and Treatment. Second Edition. Post 8vo. cloth, 10s. 6d.

FREDERICK SIMMS, M.B., M.R.C.P.

A WINTER IN PARIS: being a few Experiences and Observations of French Medical and Sanitary Matters. Fcap. 8vo. cloth, 4s.

E. B. SINCLAIR, M.D., F.K.Q.C.P., AND G. JOHNSTON, M.D., F.K.Q.C.P.

PRACTICAL MIDWIFERY: Comprising an Account of 13,748 Deliveries, which occurred in the Dublin Lying-in Hospital, during a period of Seven Years. 8vo. cloth, 10s.

J. L. SIORDET, M.B.LOND., M.R.C.P.

MENTONE IN ITS MEDICAL ASPECT. Foolscap 8vo. cloth, 2s. 6d.

ALFRED SMEE, M.R.C.S., F.R.S.

GENERAL DEBILITY AND DEFECTIVE NUTRITION; their Causes, Consequences, and Treatment. Second Edition. Fcap. 8vo. cloth, 3s. 6d.

WM. SMELLIE, M.D.

OBSTETRIC PLATES: being a Selection from the more Important and Practical Illustrations contained in the Original Work. With Anatomical and Practical Directions. 8vo. cloth, 5s.

HENRY SMITH, F.R.C.S.

I.

ON STRICTURE OF THE URETHRA. 8vo. cloth, 7s. 6d.

II.

HÆMORRHOIDS AND PROLAPSUS OF THE RECTUM: Their Pathology and Treatment, with especial reference to the use of Nitric Acid. Third Edition. Fcap. 8vo. cloth, 3s.   III.

THE SURGERY OF THE RECTUM. Lettsomian Lectures. Second Edition. Fcap. 8vo. 3s. 6d.

JOHN SMITH, M.D., F.R.C.S.EDIN.

HANDBOOK OF DENTAL ANATOMY AND SURGERY, FOR THE USE OF STUDENTS AND PRACTITIONERS. Fcap. 8vo. cloth, 3s. 6d.

J. BARKER SMITH.

PHARMACEUTICAL GUIDE TO THE FIRST AND SECOND EXAMINATIONS. Crown 8vo. cloth, 6s. 6d.

W. TYLER SMITH, M.D., F.R.C.P.

A MANUAL OF OBSTETRICS, THEORETICAL AND PRACTICAL. Illustrated with 186 Engravings. Fcap. 8vo. cloth, 12s. 6d.

JOHN SNOW, M.D.

ON CHLOROFORM AND OTHER ANÆSTHETICS: THEIR ACTION AND ADMINISTRATION. Edited, with a Memoir of the Author, by Benjamin W. Richardson, M.D. 8vo. cloth, 10s. 6d.

J. VOSE SOLOMON, F.R.O.S.

TENSION OF THE EYEBALL; GLAUCOMA: some Account of
the Operations practised in the 19th Century. 8vo. cloth, 4s.

STANHOPE TEMPLEMAN SPEER, M.D.

PATHOLOGICAL CHEMISTRY, IN ITS APPLICATION TO
THE PRACTICE OF MEDICINE. Translated from the French of MM. Becquerel
and Rodier. 8vo. cloth, reduced to 8s.

J. K. SPENDER, M.D.LOND.

A MANUAL OF THE PATHOLOGY AND TREATMENT
OF ULCERS AND CUTANEOUS DISEASES OF THE LOWER LIMBS.
8vo. cloth, 4s.

PETER SQUIRE.

I.

A COMPANION TO THE BRITISH PHARMACOPÆIA.
Seventh Edition. 8vo. cloth, 10s. 6d.   II.

THE PHARMACOPÆIAS OF THE LONDON HOSPITALS,
arranged in Groups for easy Reference and Comparison. Second Edition. 18mo.
cloth, 5s.

JOHN STEGGALL, M.D.

I.

A MEDICAL MANUAL FOR APOTHECARIES' HALL AND OTHER MEDICAL
BOARDS. Twelfth Edition. 12mo. cloth, 10s.

II.

A MANUAL FOR THE COLLEGE OF SURGEONS; intended for the Use
of Candidates for Examination and Practitioners. Second Edition. 12mo. cloth, 10s.

III.

FIRST LINES FOR CHEMISTS AND DRUGGISTS PREPARING FOR EX-
AMINATION AT THE PHARMACEUTICAL SOCIETY. Third Edition.
18mo. cloth, 3s. 6d.

WM. STOWE, M.R.C.S.

A TOXICOLOGICAL CHART, exhibiting at one view the Symptoms,
Treatment, and Mode of Detecting the various Poisons, Mineral, Vegetable, and Animal.
To which are added, concise Directions for the Treatment of Suspended Animation.
Twelfth Edition. revised. On Sheet, 2s.; mounted on Roller, 5s.

FRANCIS SUTTON, F.C.S.

A SYSTEMATIC HANDBOOK OF VOLUMETRIC ANALYSIS;
or, the Quantitative Estimation of Chemical Substances by Measure. With Engravings.
Post 8vo. cloth, 7s. 6d.

W. P. SWAIN, F.R.C.S.

INJURIES AND DISEASES OF THE KNEE-JOINT, and
their Treatment by Amputation and Excision Contrasted. Jacksonian Prize Essay.
With 36 Engravings. 8vo. cloth, 9s.

J. G. SWAYNE, M.D.

OBSTETRIC APHORISMS FOR THE USE OF STUDENTS
COMMENCING MIDWIFERY PRACTICE. With Engravings on Wood. Fourth
Edition. Fcap. 8vo. cloth, 3s. 6d.

SIR ALEXANDER TAYLOR, M.D., F.R.S.E.

THE CLIMATE OF PAU; with a Description of the Watering Places of the Pyrenees, and of the Virtues of their respective Mineral Sources in Disease. Third Edition. Post 8vo. cloth, 7s.

ALFRED S. TAYLOR, M.D., F.R.C.P., F.R.S.

I.

THE PRINCIPLES AND PRACTICE OF MEDICAL JURIS-PRUDENCE. With 176 Wood Engravings. 8vo. cloth, 28s.

II.

A MANUAL OF MEDICAL JURISPRUDENCE. Eighth Edition. With Engravings. Fcap. 8vo. cloth, 12s. 6d.

III.

ON POISONS, in relation to MEDICAL JURISPRUDENCE AND MEDICINE. Second Edition. Fcap. 8vo. cloth, 12s. 6d.

THEOPHILUS THOMPSON, M.D., F.R.C.P., F.R.S.

CLINICAL LECTURES ON PULMONARY CONSUMPTION; with additional Chapters by E. SYMES THOMPSON, M.D. With Plates. 8vo. cloth, 7s. 6d.

ROBERT THOMAS, M.D.

THE MODERN PRACTICE OF PHYSIC; exhibiting the Symptoms, Causes, Morbid Appearances, and Treatment of the Diseases of all Climates. Eleventh Edition. Revised by ALGERNON FRAMPTON, M.D. 2 vols. 8vo. cloth, 28s.

SIR HENRY THOMPSON, F.R.C.S.

I.

STRICTURE OF THE URETHRA AND URINARY FISTULÆ; their Pathology and Treatment. Jacksonian Prize Essay. With Plates. Third Edition. 8vo. cloth, 10s.

II.

THE DISEASES OF THE PROSTATE; their Pathology and Treatment. With Plates. Third Edition. 8vo. cloth, 10s.

III.

PRACTICAL LITHOTOMY AND LITHOTRITY; or, An Inquiry into the best Modes of removing Stone from the Bladder. With numerous Engravings, 8vo. cloth, 9s.

IV.

CLINICAL LECTURES ON DISEASES OF THE URINARY ORGANS. With Engravings. Second Edition. Crown 8vo. cloth, 5s.

J. C. THOROWGOOD, M.D.LOND.

NOTES ON ASTHMA; its Nature, Forms and Treatment. Crown 8vo. cloth, 4s.

J. L. W. THUDICHUM, M.D., M.R.C.P.

I.

A TREATISE ON THE PATHOLOGY OF THE URINE, Including a complete Guide to its Analysis. With Plates, 8vo. cloth, 14s.

II.

A TREATISE ON GALL STONES: their Chemistry, Pathology, and Treatment. With Coloured Plates. 8vo. cloth, 10s.

E. J. TILT, M.D., M.R.C.P.

I.

ON UTERINE AND OVARIAN INFLAMMATION, AND ON
THE PHYSIOLOGY AND DISEASES OF MENSTRUATION. Third Edition.
8vo. cloth, 12s.

II.

A HANDBOOK OF UTERINE THERAPEUTICS AND OF
DISEASES OF WOMEN.   Third Edition.   Post 8vo. cloth, 10s.

III.

THE CHANGE OF LIFE IN HEALTH AND DISEASE: a
Practical Treatise on the Nervous and other Affections incidental to Women at the Decline
of Life.   Second Edition.   8vo. cloth, 6s.

GODWIN W. TIMMS, M.D., M.R.C.P.

CONSUMPTION : its True Nature and Successful Treatment. Re-issue,
enlarged.   Crown 8vo. cloth, 10s.

ROBERT B. TODD, M.D., F.R.S.

I.

CLINICAL LECTURES ON THE PRACTICE OF MEDICINE.
New Edition, in one Volume, Edited by DR. BEALE, *8vo. cloth,* 18s.

II.

ON CERTAIN DISEASES OF THE URINARY ORGANS, AND
ON DROPSIES. Fcap. 8vo. cloth, 6s.

JOHN TOMES, F.R.S.

A MANUAL OF DENTAL SURGERY. With 208 Engravings on
Wood. Fcap. 8vo. cloth, 12s. 6d.

JAS. M. TURNBULL, M.D., M R.C.P.

I.

AN INQUIRY INTO THE CURABILITY OF CONSUMPTION,
ITS PREVENTION, AND THE PROGRESS OF IMPROVEMENT IN THE
TREATMENT. Third Edition. 8vo. cloth, 6s.

II.

A PRACTICAL TREATISE ON DISORDERS OF THE STOMACH
with FERMENTATION; and on the Causes and Treatment of Indigestion, &c.   8vo.
cloth, 6s.

R. V. TUSON, F.C.S.

A PHARMACOPŒIA ; including the Outlines of Materia Medica
and Therapeutics, for the Use of Practitioners and Students of Veterinary Medicine.
Post 8vo. cloth, 7s.

ALEXR. TWEEDIE, M.D., F.R.C.P., F.R.S.

CONTINUED FEVERS: THEIR DISTINCTIVE CHARACTERS,
PATHOLOGY, AND TREATMENT. With Coloured Plates. 8vo. cloth, 12s.

DR. UNDERWOOD.

TREATISE ON THE DISEASES OF CHILDREN. Tenth Edition,
with Additions and Corrections by HENRY DAVIES, M.D.   8vo. cloth, 15s.

VESTIGES OF THE NATURAL HISTORY OF CREATION.
Eleventh Edition.   Illustrated with 106 Engravings on Wood. 8vo. cloth, 7s. 6d.

J. L. C. SCHROEDER VAN DER KOLK.

THE PATHOLOGY AND THERAPEUTICS OF MENTAL
DISEASES. Translated by Mr. RUDALL, F.R.C.S. 8vo. cloth, 7s. 6d.

MISS VEITCH.

HANDBOOK FOR NURSES FOR THE SICK. Crown 8vo.
cloth, 2s. 6d.

ROBERT WADE, F.R.C.S.

STRICTURE OF THE URETHRA, ITS COMPLICATIONS
AND EFFECTS; a Practical Treatise on the Nature and Treatment of those
Affections. Fourth Edition. 8vo. cloth, 7s. 6d.

ADOLPHE WAHLTUCH, M.D.

A DICTIONARY OF MATERIA MEDICA AND THERA-
PEUTICS. 8vo. cloth, 15s.

J. WEST WALKER, M.B.LOND.

ON DIPHTHERIA AND DIPHTHERITIC DISEASES. Fcap.
8vo. cloth, 3s.

CHAS. WALLER, M.D.

ELEMENTS OF PRACTICAL MIDWIFERY; or, Companion to
the Lying-in Room. Fourth Edition, with Plates. Fcap. cloth, 4s. 6d.

HAYNES WALTON, F.R.C.S.

SURGICAL DISEASES OF THE EYE. With Engravings on
Wood. Second Edition. 8vo. cloth, 14s.

E. J. WARING, M.D., M.R.C.P.LOND.

I.

A MANUAL OF PRACTICAL THERAPEUTICS. Second Edition,
Revised and Enlarged. Fcap. 8vo. cloth, 12s. 6d.

II.

THE TROPICAL RESIDENT AT HOME. Letters addressed to
Europeans returning from India and the Colonies on Subjects connected with their Health
and General Welfare. Crown 8vo. cloth, 5s.

A. T. H. WATERS, M.D., F.R.C.P.

I.

DISEASES OF THE CHEST. CONTRIBUTIONS TO THEIR
CLINICAL HISTORY, PATHOLOGY, AND TREATMENT. With Plates.
8vo. cloth, 12s. 6d.

II.

THE ANATOMY OF THE HUMAN LUNG. The Prize Essay
to which the Fothergillian Gold Medal was awarded by the Medical Society of London.
Post 8vo. cloth, 6s. 6d.

III.

RESEARCHES ON THE NATURE, PATHOLOGY, AND
TREATMENT OF EMPHYSEMA OF THE LUNGS, AND ITS RELA-
TIONS WITH OTHER DISEASES OF THE CHEST. With Engravings. 8vo.

ALLAN WEBB, M.D., F.R.C.S.L.

THE SURGEON'S READY RULES FOR OPERATIONS IN
SURGERY. Royal 8vo. cloth, 10s. 6d.

J. SOELBERG WELLS.

I.

A TREATISE ON THE DISEASES OF THE EYE. With
Coloured Plates and Wood Engravings. 8vo. cloth, 24s.

II.

ON LONG, SHORT, AND WEAK SIGHT, and their Treatment by
the Scientific Use of Spectacles. Third Edition. With Plates. 8vo. cloth, 6s.

T. SPENCER WELLS, F.R.C.S.

SCALE OF MEDICINES FOR MERCHANT VESSELS.
With Observations on the Means of Preserving the Health of Seamen, &c. &c.
Seventh Thousand. Fcap. 8vo. cloth, 3s. 6d.

CHARLES WEST, M.D., F.R.C.P.

LECTURES ON THE DISEASES OF WOMEN. Third Edition.
8vo. cloth, 16s.

J. A. WHEELER.

HAND-BOOK OF ANATOMY FOR STUDENTS OF THE
FINE ARTS. With Engravings on Wood. Fcap. 8vo., 2s. 6d.

JAMES WHITEHEAD, M.D., M.R.C.P.

ON THE TRANSMISSION FROM PARENT TO OFFSPRING
OF SOME FORMS OF DISEASE, AND OF MORBID TAINTS AND
TENDENCIES. Second Edition. 8vo. cloth, 10s. 6d.

C. J. B. WILLIAMS, M.D., F.R.C.P., F.R.S.

PRINCIPLES OF MEDICINE : An Elementary View of the Causes,
Nature, Treatment, Diagnosis, and Prognosis, of Disease. With brief Remarks on
Hygienics, or the Preservation of Health. The Third Edition. 8vo. cloth, 15s.

FORBES WINSLOW, M.D., D.C.L.OXON.

OBSCURE DISEASES OF THE BRAIN AND MIND.
Fourth Edition. Carefully Revised. Post 8vo. cloth, 10s. 6d.

T. A. WISE, M.D., F.R.C.P.EDIN.

REVIEW OF THE HISTORY OF MEDICINE AMONG
ASIATIC NATIONS. Two Vols. 8vo. cloth, 16s.

ERASMUS WILSON, F.R.C.S., F.R.S.

I.

THE ANATOMIST'S VADE-MECUM: A SYSTEM OF HUMAN
ANATOMY. With numerous Illustrations on Wood. Eighth Edition. Foolscap 8vo. cloth, 12s. 6d.

II.

ON DISEASES OF THE SKIN: A SYSTEM OF CUTANEOUS
MEDICINE. Sixth Edition. 8vo. cloth, 18s.
THE SAME WORK; illustrated with finely executed Engravings on Steel, accurately coloured. 8vo. cloth, 36s.

III.

HEALTHY SKIN: A Treatise on the Management of the Skin and Hair
in relation to Health. Seventh Edition. Foolscap 8vo. 2s. 6d.

IV.

PORTRAITS OF DISEASES OF THE SKIN. Folio. Fasciculi I.
to XII., completing the Work. 20s. each. The Entire Work, half morocco, £13.

V.

THE STUDENT'S BOOK OF CUTANEOUS MEDICINE AND
DISEASES OF THE SKIN. Post 8vo. cloth, 8s. 6d.

VI.

LECTURES ON EKZEMA AND EKZEMATOUS AFFEC-
TIONS; with an Introduction on the General Pathology of the Skin, and an Appendix of Essays and Cases. 8vo. cloth, 10s. 6d.

VII.

ON SYPHILIS, CONSTITUTIONAL AND HEREDITARY;
AND ON SYPHILITIC ERUPTIONS. With Four Coloured Plates. 8vo. cloth, 16s.

VIII.

A THREE WEEKS' SCAMPER THROUGH THE SPAS OF
GERMANY AND BELGIUM, with an Appendix on the Nature and Uses of Mineral Waters. Post 8vo. cloth, 6s. 6d.

IX.

THE EASTERN OR TURKISH BATH: its History, Revival in
Britain, and Application to the Purposes of Health. Foolscap 8vo., 2s.

G. C. WITTSTEIN.

PRACTICAL PHARMACEUTICAL CHEMISTRY: An Explanation
of Chemical and Pharmaceutical Processes, with the Methods of Testing the Purity of the Preparations, deduced from Original Experiments. Translated from the Second German Edition, by STEPHEN DARBY. 18mo. cloth, 6s.

HENRY G. WRIGHT, M.D., M.R.C.P.

I.

UTERINE DISORDERS: their Constitutional Influence and Treatment.
8vo. cloth, 7s. 6d.

II.

HEADACHES; their Causes and their Cure. Fourth Edition. Fcap. 8vo.
2s. 6d.

CHURCHILL'S SERIES OF MANUALS.

Fcap. 8vo. cloth, 12s. 6d. each.

"We here give Mr. Churchill public thanks for the positive benefit conferred on the Medical Profession, by the series of beautiful and cheap Manuals which bear his imprint."— *British and Foreign Medical Review.*

AGGREGATE SALE, 154,000 COPIES.

ANATOMY. With numerous Engravings. Eighth Edition. By ERASMUS WILSON, F.R.C.S., F.R.S.

BOTANY. With numerous Engravings. By ROBERT BENTLEY, F.L.S., Professor of Botany, King's College. and to the Pharmaceutical Society.

CHEMISTRY. With numerous Engravings. Tenth Edition, 14s. By GEORGE FOWNES. F.R.S., H. BENCE JONES, M.D., F.R.S., and HENRY WATTS, B.A., F.R.S.

DENTAL SURGERY. With numerous Engravings. By JOHN TOMES, F.R.S.

EYE, DISEASES OF. With coloured Plates and Engravings on Wood. By C. MACNAMARA.

MATERIA MEDICA. With numerous Engravings. Fifth Edition. By J. FORBES ROYLE, M.D., F.R.S., and F. W. HEADLAND, M.D., F.R.C.P.

MEDICAL JURISPRUDENCE. With numerous Engravings. Eighth Edition. By ALFRED SWAINE TAYLOR, M.D., F.R.S.

PRACTICE OF MEDICINE. Second Edition. By G. HILARO BARLOW, M.D., M.A.

The MICROSCOPE and its REVELATIONS. With numerous Plates and Engravings. Fourth Edition. By W. B. CARPENTER, M.D., F.R.S.

NATURAL PHILOSOPHY. With numerous Engravings. Sixth Edition. By CHARLES BROOKE, M.B., M.A., F.R.S. *Based on the Work of the late Dr. Golding Bird.*

OBSTETRICS. With numerous Engravings. By W. TYLER SMITH, M.D., F.R.C.P.

OPHTHALMIC MEDICINE and SURGERY. With coloured Plates and Engravings on Wood. Third Edition. By T. WHARTON JONES, F.R.C.S., F.R.S.

PATHOLOGICAL ANATOMY. With numerous Engravings. By C. HANDFIELD JONES, M.B., F.R.S., and E. H. SIEVEKING, M.D., F.R.C.P.

PHYSIOLOGY. With numerous Engravings. Fourth Edition. By WILLIAM B. CARPENTER, M.D., F.R.S.

POISONS. Second Edition. By ALFRED SWAINE TAYLOR, M.D., F.R.S.

PRACTICAL ANATOMY. With numerous Engravings. Second Edition. By CHRISTOPHER HEATH, F.R.C.S.

PRACTICAL SURGERY. With numerous Engravings. Fourth Edition. By Sir WILLIAM FERGUSSON, Bart., F.R.C.S., F.R.S.

THERAPEUTICS. Second Edition. By E. J. Waring, M.D., M.R.C.P.

www.ingramcontent.com/pod-product-compliance
Lightning Source LLC
Chambersburg PA
CBHW030115030726
47498CB00007B/2401